THE ARIZONA DUI HANDBOOK

Scott David Stewart, Esq.
and
Colin Bell, Esq.

An Imprint of Stewart Law Group
www.ArizonaLawGroup.com

THE ARIZONA DUI HANDBOOK

Scott David Stewart, Esq.
and
Colin Bell, Esq.

An Imprint of Stewart Law Group
www.ArizonaLawGroup.com

Published in 2017 by Stewart Law Group USA

• 777 E Thomas Rd Ste 210, Phoenix AZ 85014 •
• 1490 S Price Rd Ste 212, Chandler AZ 85286 •
• 17470 N Pacesetter Way, Scottsdale AZ 85255 •
• 14050 N 83rd Ave Ste 290, Peoria AZ 85381 •
• 2929 N Power Rd Ste 101, Mesa AZ 85215 •
• 20325 N 51st Ave Ste 134, Glendale AZ 85308 •
• 1166 E Warner Rd Ste 101U, Gilbert AZ 85296 •

www.arizonalawgroup.com

FIRST EDITION

ISBN 978-0-9886052-8-2

For information please write:

Stewart Law Group
777 E Thomas Rd Ste 210
Phoenix AZ 85014

Legal Disclaimer

The general information in this book is not, nor is it intended to be, specific legal advice. You should consult an attorney for specific legal advice regarding your individual situation.

This book is provided as a general reference work and is for informational purposes only. You are advised to check for changes to current law and to consult with a qualified attorney on any legal issue. The receipt of or use of this book does not create an attorney-client relationship with Stewart Law Group or any of its attorneys.

Because this book was prepared for a general readership, without investigation into the facts of each particular case, it is not legal advice. Neither Stewart Law Group nor any of its attorneys has an attorney-client relationship with you. The thoughts and commentary about the law contained in this book are provided merely as a public service and do not constitute solicitation or legal advice.

While we endeavored to provide accurate information in this book, we cannot guarantee that the material provided herein is accurate, adequate, or complete. This general legal information is provided on an 'as is' basis. We make no warranties and disclaim liability for damages resulting from its use. Legal advice must be tailored to the specific circumstances of each case and laws are constantly changing, so nothing provided in this book should be used as a substitute for the advice of competent counsel. The material in this book may be considered advertising under applicable rules.

Contents

Acknowledgements

Thanks to those who made helpful suggestions and, in their own way, contributed to The Arizona DUI Handbook. To Laura Valade, J.D., for her research and editing which was instrumental in bringing this project to fruition. To the attorneys with Stewart Law Group whose contributions to the legal profession are valued and celebrated. Finally, to my family for their unflagging support in my taking on yet another book writing project.

INTRODUCTION

This Arizona DUI handbook is an easy-to-read guide for anyone arrested for driving under the influence in Arizona and a great starting point for a spouse, family member, or close friend of the person facing a DUI trial.

Being charged with DUI can be very frightening. People worry about what might happen. "What if there's a criminal trial?" "Who will represent me?" "What if I'm convicted?" "How can I care for my family from a jail cell?" "How much will I pay in criminal fines?" "What are the consequences of having a criminal record?" "Could I lose my job?" "Will my driver's license be suspended?" "What happens to my insurance rates?"

What You'll Take Away From This Book

For easy navigation, we divided this book into eight chapters. For the best reader experience, we recommend reading the book in its entirety from beginning to end. Then go back to the chapters that are most important given your concerns and situation.

Briefly, here is what you will take away from this book:

Chapter 1 begins at the beginning — the police stop. This chapter sets the stage for the DUI case. When do police have reasonable suspicion to stop the vehicle? Did the police set up a sobriety checkpoint? Is probable cause important to DUI arrest? What are Miranda warnings? These and many more questions are answered in the opening chapter.

Chapter 2 covers field sobriety tests during the police stop. Did police use non-standardized field sobriety tests? Does the arresting officer testify at trial on driver's performance of field sobriety tests? How do weather conditions, lighting, time of day, and road conditions impact field sobriety testing? What if the driver refused to take the test?

In **Chapter 3**, learn about BAC and testing for drugs and alcohol in blood, breath, urine, or other bodily fluids. How long does it take to sober up after drinking an alcoholic beverage? Can a driver using prescribed drugs or medical marijuana still be charged with DUI? Are commercial drivers held to different standards of BAC? Do charges differ for drivers below the legal drinking age? What is Arizona's implied consent law? What DUI crimes can be charged under Arizona law? How does extreme DUI differ from aggravated DUI? Are all DUIs misdemeanors?

In **Chapter 4**, learn what happens following driver arrest. How does the owner get the vehicle out of impound? This is followed in **Chapter 5** with a description of each court proceeding in the DUI criminal process through sentencing and appeal, both for felony and misdemeanor DUI. What are plea negotiations all about?

Chapter 6 walks through the five steps in a DUI trial. What is the difference between a jury trial and bench trial? What happens if there is a mistrial? How does the trial proceed? If the verdict is guilty or the sentence is too harsh, then could an appeal be filed? Does Arizona's victims' bill of rights have an impact on sentencing? What is self-surrender to the jail all about?

In **Chapter 7**, the driver's license suspension and MVD hearings are covered. How do MVD proceedings differ from the criminal case? Can a private attorney represent the driver before the MVD? What happens after license suspension? How can one obtain a restricted license? This chapter explains license reinstatement, too, and what could happen when a driver is arrested for DUI on suspended license.

Lastly, **Chapter 8** goes through a checklist of what to look for in a DUI defense attorney. With everything on the line, choose a legal defense team wisely!

Who should read this book? Any adult who has been arrested for DUI in Arizona needs to read this book. We don't delve into juvenile justice issues, but drivers under the age of 18 will still find each DUI chapter worth reading.

There could be additional offenses that are related to drunk driving, but are not covered in this book. These include operating a boat under the influence (A.R.S. § 5-395) and operating an aircraft under the influence (A.R.S. § 28-8282). Trust that a DUI defense lawyer's representation is essential against those potential charges, too.

Just one more thing before getting started. The materials on these pages are likely to spark more questions about DUI and related offenses, such as drug possession. We have additional resources on our firm website at www.arizonalawgroup.com/criminal-defense/DUI. For specific legal advice, though, always consult an experienced DUI criminal defense lawyer. We hope you'll call us first. We know precisely how to help you through the challenges ahead. It's what we do.

1

Police Stops, DUI Checkpoints, Things to Discuss with Your Lawyer

The Police Stop

Every DUI begins with a police stop based on a police officer's reasonable suspicion that the driver is engaging in a criminal act (DUI). That is the point at which police open the report and start gathering evidence of a crime. The officer is making observations, compiling a police report, and already thinking in terms of testifying later at MVD hearing on driver's license suspension and at trial, should those come to pass. At trial, the arresting officer will be the state's key witness. Remember, the police are always building their case against you.

Assume that every law enforcement officer has received DUI training and has DUI arrest experience, even if a Rookie. Police do make mistakes. They sometimes fail to follow official police procedure. They sometimes fail to conduct themselves according to police regulations.

To protect clients' civil rights, defense attorneys investigate any possibility that police made mistakes, deviated from standard police procedures, or failed to conduct themselves as police regulations require. At the traffic stop, for example, the officer obtained driver's consent to breath testing, but did not properly instruct the driver on how to blow into the breath testing device (keep blowing into Intoxilyzer so sufficient air is expelled for accurate reading). The defense can challenge the breath test because it was not performed according to standard police procedure. The defense attorney should know standard police procedure and be prepared to pounce on any deviation.

Unjustified Traffic Stop Can Result in Unlawful Arrest

Generally, an unlawful arrest follows an unjustified police stop. Why was the driver stopped by police in the first place? The illegal traffic stop could lead to unlawful DUI arrest, a defense worthy of dismissal in many cases.

For a DUI charge to have any teeth, two things need to happen. First, police must have reasonable suspicion of criminal activity (not necessarily impaired driving) or observe a traffic violation in order to stop the driver. Second, police must have probable cause to arrest the driver. Events must occur in that order or the arrest is unlawful and charges may be dropped.

Police Must Have Reasonable Suspicion to Stop the Driver

To justify the police stop, Arizona law enforcement must have a reasonable suspicion that the driver is committing a crime or, in the alternative, police must actually have observed the driver violate traffic laws. Reasonable suspicion is an objective standard.

This means police must have had an objective reason

to stop the driver (for example, the driver ran a red light, operated a vehicle at night without headlights, or proceeded the wrong way on a Phoenix one-way street). Whether police had reasonable suspicion is a question of law for the judge to determine; this is not a question of fact for the jury.

Unlike the movies and as experienced and enthusiastic as the officer may be, strong intuition or a gut-feeling that the driver might be doing something criminal does not justify a traffic stop. If the police stop was unjustified, then the DUI arrest that followed is likewise unlawful.

Reasons Why Police Stop Vehicles

There are two basic reasons why law enforcement stop drivers on Arizona roadways and both require police observations. The first involves a traffic violation (not using your blinker, speeding, or passing in a "no passing" zone). The second involves the police witnessing some indication, or cues, of driver impairment.

Objective indicators of driver impairment, called "cues" by the National Highway Traffic Safety Administration (NHTSA),[1] could, in combination, give police reasonable suspicion to believe a DUI crime is being committed. Those cues include:

Problems maintaining proper lane position

1. Weaving and weaving across lane lines
2. Straddling a lane line
3. Swerving
4. Turning with a wide radius
5. Drifting
6. Almost striking a vehicle or other object

Speed and braking problems

1. Stopping problems (too far, too short, too jerky)
2. Accelerating or decelerating for no apparent reason
3. Varying speed
4. Slow speed (10+ mph under the speed limit)

Vigilance problems

1. Driving in opposing lanes or wrong way on a one-way
2. Slow response to traffic signals
3. Slow or failure to respond to officer's signals
4. Stopping in lane for no apparent reason
5. Driving without headlights at night
6. Failure to signal or signal inconsistent with action

Judgment problems

1. Following too closely
2. Improper or unsafe lane change
3. Illegal or improper turn (too fast, too jerky, too sharp)
4. Driving on other than the designated roadway
5. Stopping inappropriately in response to officer
6. Inappropriate or unusual behavior (throwing, arguing)
7. Appearing to be impaired

These cues are not proof of driving drunk, but they could justify the police stop. Why? Reasonable suspicion is based on police observing the driver doing one or more cues on the NHTSA list. This is something the arresting officer will be questioned about under oath as the state's key witness in the DUI trial.

How might this impact your case? Your DUI defense lawyer will question each cue relied on by police and investigate whether police really did witness bad driving (or did the officer embellish on the truth or exaggerate to justify an otherwise illegal traffic stop?). Weaving across lane lines is not proof of intoxication, drivers sometimes do this for completely sober reasons (dropped something on the floor and was reaching around to find it). Some vehicles do not track straight going down the road, making it appear that the driver is causing the vehicle to wander within the lane. The driver simply failed to signal before turning, just a one-off that can happen to anyone. Defense strategy includes offering other explanations to the jury that give a perfectly legitimate excuse for what might otherwise be interpreted as a DUI cue.

What happens immediately after the stop? The NHTSA lists "post stop cues" giving police reason to investigate possible DUI with field sobriety testing or other tests (discussed later):

1. Difficulty with motor vehicle controls
2. Difficulty exiting the vehicle
3. Fumbling with driver's license or registration
4. Repeating questions or comments
5. Swaying, unsteady, or balance problems
6. Leaning on the vehicle or other object
7. Slurred speech
8. Slow to respond to officer or officer must repeat
9. Providing incorrect information, changes answers
10. Odor of alcoholic beverage from the driver

There may be a number of perfectly legal reasons for why the driver might appear to be under the influence, but not be. The driver's face seemed red or flushed (person has skin rosacea, a sunburn, or finished a boot-camp work-out at the park only minutes before). The driver appeared poorly groomed (person is a laborer who just got off work or is a student who has been up all night studying for final exams). The driver stumbled or swayed getting out of the car (person tripped over a pot-hole or lost balance at the edge of the pavement). The driver had bloodshot, half-closed, watery eyes (person has a cold or allergies or is fatigued having just worked a double-shift). Defense strategy includes providing any number of explanations (other than drug or alcohol use) to the fact-finder that, if true, could explain away the NHTSA cues.

DUI Arrest at Sobriety Checkpoint

Did the arrest take place at a DUI checkpoint? You're not alone. On 14 nights in December, New Year's Eve, Fourth of July weekend, St. Patrick's day, Cinco de Mayo, Memorial Day weekend, Thanksgiving weekend, Halloween, and Super Bowl Sunday, for example, DUI checkpoints with roadblocks are set-up by police on I-10 and other busy highways around Arizona. Those celebratory events mean police have a good chance of catching an intoxicated driver even though the person has not exhibited any impairment while driving.

How do DUI checkpoints work? With a roadblock, all drivers funnel through the checkpoint and are briefly interviewed by police. Most drivers are waved through, others are detained further. Detained drivers may then be subjected to field sobriety tests and blood, breath, or urine testing. Drivers can be arrested for DUI. The sobriety checkpoint, then, is a golden opportunity for police to stop a sea of drivers in the hope of catching a live one. Police save money and resources implementing DUI checkpoints, but at a cost to liberty interests of the general public.

As already noted, law enforcement must have reasonable suspicion to justify a police stop. Why, then, is it permissible for police to stop any or all drivers with a roadblock in an attempt to winnow out a few potentially impaired drivers when police cannot stop a lone driver without reasonable suspicion of criminal activity?

The legality of Arizona's DUI checkpoints was held to be constitutional in State v. Superior Court In and For Pima County, 691 P.2d 1073 (Ariz. 1984). In that decision, the Arizona Supreme Court balanced the DUI problem and danger, against the intrusion on public liberty. The Arizona Supreme Court upheld police roadblocks:

> *"Given the gravity of the problem, a compelling need for the state to take strong action against drunk drivers, and the minimal intru-*

sion created by these stops, we hold the stops in this case passed constitutional muster."

In 1990, the U.S. Supreme Court upheld the constitutionality of DUI checkpoints (balancing the substantial government interest in enforcing DUI laws against the burden of checkpoints on individual liberty) as reasonable searches and seizures under the Fourth Amendment to the U.S. Constitution. Michigan Dept. of State Police v. Sitz, 496 U.S. 444 (1990).

Importantly, because DUI checkpoints are an intrusion on fundamental liberty interests, police must follow specific guidelines. Defense attorneys investigate any police violations in obtaining government permission to set up the roadblock, police misconduct or failure to follow standard procedures in operating the sobriety checkpoint, and any inconsistency in how police treated arrestees, among other things.

DUI arrest at a sobriety checkpoint does not diminish the person's civil rights which, if violated, could result in dismissal of the charges. Talk to a lawyer.

Warrantless Search and Reasonable Suspicion Motion

Most DUI arrests occur in the absence of a warrant. Under the Fourth Amendment, search and seizure includes arrest (seizure of the person). Any warrantless search and seizure is presumed to be unconstitutional.

If a warrantless search resulted in the driver's arrest, then defense counsel may file a pre-trial reasonable suspicion motion. By doing so, the defendant presents a prima facie case (evidence) that the search was invalid and that any and all evidence obtained from that illegal search should be suppressed. The burden is on the state to prove, by a preponderance of the evidence, that some exception to the Fourth Amendment applies allowing the evidence. If the state does not carry its burden, then the evidence should be suppressed.

Police Must Have Probable Cause to Arrest

We discussed that police must have reasonable suspicion or observe a traffic violation to initiate a traffic stop. This is a question of law for the judge to determine. It may be that the driver is cited for a moving violation, and that's it. But if a driver is to be taken into police custody on suspicion of DUI, then law enforcement must have probable cause to arrest. That standard — probable cause to arrest — has substantial legal meaning under the Fourth Amendment of the U.S. Constitution and under state law.

Unless police have a warrant to arrest the driver, probable cause to arrest must exist or the arrest is unlawful. If the arrest is unlawful, then the DUI charge must be dismissed. An arrest under suspicion of DUI, requires police have probable cause.

In a nutshell, probable cause to arrest means that, under the facts and circumstances available at the moment, police had a reasonable belief that a crime was committed. In legalese, probable cause to arrest is defined as:

> *"[S]uch a state of facts as would lead a man of ordinary caution or prudence to believe and consciously entertain a strong suspicion of guilt."*
>
> *State v. Emery, 131 Ariz. 493 (1982).*

When the defense challenges the constitutionality of the DUI arrest in court, having filed a probable cause motion, the judge must determine whether police had probable cause to arrest because the facts and circumstances within the officers' knowledge at the moment the driver was arrested would "warrant a man of reasonable caution in the belief" that a crime was committed. Carroll v. U.S., 45 S.Ct. 280 (1924).

Be mindful that while a police stop is underway officers are assessing all the facts and circumstances to determine whether they have probable cause to arrest the driver for operating a vehicle while impaired even in the slightest. (More about probable cause in preliminary hearings later.)

Did police have probable cause to arrest? Every U.S. citizen has the right to be free from unlawful arrest under the Fourth Amendment to the U.S. Constitution. Defendant's attorney will review every aspect of what happened leading up to the arrest to determine whether police had probable cause. A probable cause motion to dismiss gets the case thrown out if the judge rules police unlawfully arrested the driver without probable cause.

Miranda Warnings After DUI Arrest

An arrest can occur at the traffic stop, police headquarters, even a DUI checkpoint. After the arrest and before questioning (interrogation) can begin, police must give Miranda warnings to the driver in custody (who is unable to leave).

Miranda warnings relate to testimonial evidence — what the driver said or communicated to police. For example, when asked by police, "On a scale from 1 to 10, how drunk are you?" the driver says, "We had a couple drinks at the bar, but no way I'm that drunk!" Or answers, "I'm an 8." Answers like these are testimonial, incriminating, and could be used at trial as admissions of guilt. "You have the right to remain silent," use that right to protect against self-incrimination!

Generally, driver's statements and answers to police questions given before arrest are admissible at trial. By comparison, the driver's statements and answers to police questions given after arrest are inadmissible if Miranda warnings were not given first. Remember this: Once in police custody, any of driver's answers to police questions are inadmissible at trial as unlawfully obtained testimonial evidence if the suspect was not given Miranda warnings first. The order of events is crucial!

Always cooperate with police, but that can be done without answering questions. Always remember that the police have a job to do: Building a case against you. Request and keep requesting to have a lawyer present during any questioning!

These are the four Miranda warnings (clip and save!):

Miranda Warnings:

1. You have the right to remain silent.
2. Anything you say can and will be used against you in a court of law.
3. You have the right to the presence of an attorney to assist you prior to questioning, and to be with you during questioning, if you so desire.
4. If you cannot afford an attorney, you have the right to have an attorney appointed to you prior to questioning.

DUI Defense

Not all drivers arrested for DUI should face criminal charges or, if charged, be convicted. Every DUI defendant is presumed to be innocent until proven guilty beyond a reasonable doubt. Those are not idle words. That is our criminal justice system.

Because drivers accused of DUI are sometimes convinced (or convince themselves) that they have no hope of winning their case, they give up without a fight and never present an adequate defense. They accept plea agreements when they could have won at trial. They hire inexperienced lawyers at a reduced rate believing they are going to lose regardless. Many people attempt to save money by not hiring a lawyer, which is worse. They do not know their rights, they do not understand where and when those rights apply, and because they do not aggressively assert their rights, the results are often unfair, unjust, and sadly permanent.

Your DUI defense begins with you. This book gives you the tools you need to start asserting your constitutionally protected rights and prepare for criminal court proceedings. We strongly recommend, however, that you hire an experienced DUI defense lawyer immediately. If hiring a private attorney is just not possible, then seek legal representation through the Public Defender's Office. Do it now.

Pre-Charge Representation

Arrested for DUI? Get your defense attorney on the case as soon as possible. All too often, people are in denial about the seriousness of DUIs in Arizona law. Many are under the mistaken impression that there is ample time to make decisions, shop for a lawyer, and get things straightened out. Well, there isn't much time and the court will get things straightened out for you if you don't act aggressively in your own defense.

Additionally, the DUI might not be the only charge. Other offenses may be under investigation by law enforcement, such as endangerment, possession of stolen goods, or possession of dangerous drugs. Is there a chance the state's investigation may be ongoing? Then immediately obtain pre-charge legal representation by hiring a criminal defense lawyer for all upcoming legal proceedings.

Burden of Proof and Admissibility of Evidence

To obtain a conviction, the state has the burden of proving every element of the crime beyond a reasonable doubt. This is true with every criminal offense, not just DUI prosecution. Satisfying this burden of proof requires presentation of evidence. Not all evidence is admissible at trial against the defendant. The defense attorney's job includes challenging the state's evidence, whatever that may be — breath test, blood test, field sobriety test, driver's admission to drinking, or other. The attorney's years of DUI defense experience and rate of success matters greatly in this.

Is the test admissible as evidence at trial? If yes, then what is the weight of that evidence? Evidence obtained in unlawful arrest, mishandled test samples, miscalibrated testing equipment (Intoxilyzer, for example), contradictory police testimony, these are the types of evidentiary challenges a defense lawyer raises. If the judge rules evidence inadmissible, then there may be insufficient evidence remaining to uphold a conviction. The end result of the criminal proceedings could be dismissal of DUI charges, a not-guilty verdict, or an overturned conviction on appeal.

That the state has blood alcohol concentration (BAC)[2] test results, for instance, showing a driver exceeded the legal limit of 0.08% BAC does not mean the blood test is admissible as evidence against that defendant in court.

Consider this scenario: Driver consents to a blood test which comes back 0.10% BAC. Driver is charged with a first time DUI misdemeanor. Under oath, the arresting officer testifies that the blood test kit used was stored in the officer's motorcycle saddlebag for several months, the seal could have been damaged, and the test kit might have been exposed to the air and desert heat. The defense challenges the test as unreliable; the judge agrees and excludes the test. Because the strength of the state's case is so severely weakened without the blood test as proof of driver's BAC having exceeded the legal limit (0.08%), the case is dismissed for insufficiency of evidence that could lead to a conviction.

Although merely an example, this scenario is not a rare occurrence. Understand that there are many reasons why offered evidence is ruled inadmissible and, once excluded, cannot be considered by the finder of fact at trial (judge in a bench trial; jury in a jury trial).

CHAPTER ENDNOTES

1. NHTSA is part of the U.S. Department of Transportation. The Visual Detection of DWI Motorists is for law enforcement training. See www.NHTSA.gov for more details.

2. Although Arizona's DUI statute refers specifically to "alcohol concentration" (AC) in the blood, we use "blood alcohol concentration" (BAC) meaning the same.

2

Undergoing Field Sobriety Tests During Police Stop

With a potential DUI, there's a good chance the driver stopped by police will be asked to take a few tests – right then and there. Field sobriety tests (FST's) have been around for decades. They are administered by law enforcement during traffic stops to help police objectively observe drivers. How someone performs each field sobriety test could give the officer probable cause to arrest (or not).

What general purpose do field sobriety tests, or FSTs, serve? They are intended to assist police in deciding whether or not the person may have been intoxicated or impaired while driving or in actual control of a motor vehicle. FSTs may indicate alcohol intoxication, but they are not proof of it.

While law enforcement often rely on FSTs to determine driver impairment, this does not mean these field tests are fool proof. Many factors influence FSTs and could erode usefulness. Attempting the walk-and-turn and then one-leg-stand on a mountain road of loose gravel during a stormy monsoon night, for example, while counting backwards by subtracting in threes, all while wearing fashion heels could challenge the most sober among us. Field sobriety tests are far from infallible!

Additionally, not all field sobriety tests are equal in the law. In Arizona, police should only implement standardized field sobriety tests (SFST) validated by the National Highway Traffic Safety Administration (NHTSA). If the test administered by police was not NHTSA-validated or SFSTs were administered but under difficult conditions where environmental, terrain, or traffic situations are unsuitable, then the tests may be challenged by the defense later on.

3 Standard Field Sobriety Tests

In Arizona DUI law, the three standardized field sobriety tests that are most commonly given to impaired driving suspects are:

1. Horizontal Gaze Nystagmus Test (HGN)
2. Walk-and-Turn Test (WAT)
3. One-Leg-Stand Test (OLS)

Horizontal Gaze Nystagmus Test (HGN) is used to detect minute, involuntary, side-to-side eye movements that might indicate alcohol intoxication, among other things. Nystagmus is a medical term meaning involuntary eye movement — there are over 80 types of nystagmus!

Did the arresting officer hold up a pen and instruct the driver to follow it with the eyes side-to-side, without moving the head? Was the driver wearing glasses during the HGN test or have any medical conditions that could affect results?

HGN test results can give police probable cause to arrest the driver. At trial, however, HGN test results can only be used for two purposes. One, to corroborate a chemical test of blood, breath, urine, or saliva. Two, in the absence of a chemical test, the "HGN test results may be admitted only for the purpose of permitting the officer to testify that, based on his training and experience, the results indicated possible neurological dysfunction, one cause of which could be alcohol ingestion." A foundation for the officer's testimony is limited to education, training, and experience in administering HGN tests.[1]

Walk-and-Turn Test (WAT) is used to observe

the person's balance, ability to understand verbal instructions, and agility in executing those instructions. The test deliberately divides the person's attention. Why? Because someone intoxicated or impaired may have difficulty multi-tasking.

With hands at one's side, the person is instructed to place right foot in front of left, heel-to-toe, take nine steps while counting aloud and looking down at his or her feet, and then pivot on one foot and return the same way. Was the test conducted in a sufficiently roomy area on a surface that was reasonably flat, non-slippery, dry, hard, and level?

One-Leg-Stand Test (OLS) is another balance, capacity, and agility test which also divides attention. With arms at the side, the person is instructed to raise one foot six inches off the ground and, while looking at the raised foot, count for 30 seconds.

For the person with balance problems or health issues that affect strength, this could be a difficult task to accomplish. To regain balance, intoxicated or not, people often hop, sway, lift their arms, or put the raised foot back down on the ground. Was the driver over the age of 65, or was suffering from inner ear balance problems, or was more than 50 pounds overweight?

Each SFST must be administered according to NHTSA standards, too. Any improperly administered test provides results that are neither scientific nor reliable and should be challenged by defendant's attorney. Furthermore, many drivers simply are poor candidates for SFSTs because of age, disability, or health concern. Those individuals should not even be asked by police to complete the walk-and-turn, one-leg-stand, or HGN with head tilted back.

Non-Standard Field Sobriety Tests Are Invalid

Now take a look at some non-standard field sobriety tests. Non-standardized FSTs are not validated by NHTSA. Nevertheless, police still sometimes use the following FSTs:

- **Vertical Gaze Nystagmus** (VGN) is another eye-movement test, only the driver looks up-and-down instead of side-to-side.
- **Romberg Test** (Romberg Modified or Modified-Position-of-Attention Test) is used to observe the person's balance and ability to follow instructions. It's another multi-tasking exercise. Did police instruct the driver to stand with feet together, arms at the side, with eyes closed and head tilted back while counting backwards?
- **Finger-to-Nose Test** is used to test balance and ability to follow instructions. Did police instruct

the driver to keep feet together, arms outstretched to the side with eyes closed, and to touch the tip of the index finger to the tip of the nose, alternating from right to left hand? (In a test of his sanity, not sobriety, Mr. Clause flawlessly performed the finger-to-nose test in the film Miracle on 34th Street.)

- **Alphabet Test or Counting Test** serve little purpose in assessing impairment or intoxication. Did police instruct the driver to say the alphabet backwards (something any person might struggle with)?

No field sobriety test, not even standardized ones, are 100% reliable. Generally, these tests are not accurate predictors of driver intoxication or impairment. For example, a person could easily stumble during the walk-and-turn on a stretch of uneven, poorly-lit roadway, making it appear that he or she is impaired. Roadside test results neither prove nor disprove driver impairment or sobriety. But that does not mean the driver's refusal to perform the tests is without consequences. At trial, that refusal could be inferred evidence of guilt.

Driver's Refusal to Perform Standardized Field Sobriety Tests

Refusing a standardized field sobriety test can come with a price. Assuming police lawfully requested the SFST before the driver refused, the state will offer the driver's refusal at trial as proof of DUI guilt. Here's why.

A person's refusal to take any SFST during the police stop is not constitutionally protected by the Fifth Amendment privilege against self-incrimination. At trial, that refusal to perform the SFST may be admissible as evidence of guilt. Even though the driver's refusal to perform SFSTs was because performing the test would obviate intoxication or impairment, there is no invoking the privilege against self-incrimination. That's the law.

Portable Breath Test Results Are Inadmissible

There is another test law enforcement frequently use at police stops – the portable breath test. PBTs are unreliable. They should never form the sole basis of a DUI charge and should never be admissible as scientific evidence of blood alcohol content (BAC) in court.

Why do police use PBTs? When police have reasonable suspicion of driver intoxication, a preliminary breath test with a PBT unit may be used before arrest. A.R.S. § 28-1322. Only standard breath analyzer equipment properly calibrated and maintained can provide scientifically accurate BAC evidence in court!

As a preliminary test, the PBT assists police in deciding whether additional testing should be done. PBT results should only be used to put drivers in the BAC ball park, nothing more.

The state cannot use PBT results as evidence of BAC in court. For example, the arresting officer testifies that PBT results (inadmissible test results — unscientific, unreliable) indicated high BAC so police administered an Intoxilyzer breath test (admissible test results — scientific, reliable). That scenario is a far cry from using PBT results as direct proof of intoxication at trial. Talk to a lawyer!

With breath testing, the driver is repeat-tested to confirm the initial Intoxilyzer BAC test results. The BAC on the consecutive test must be within 0.020% of the first. If the second test is not within 0.020% of the first, then the officer must retest the driver until results are within 0.020% of the first. When BAC test results cannot be confirmed in this way, the DUI defense attorney should file a motion to suppress.

Evidentiary issues in DUI cases are often numerous

and highly technical in nature. Which is why, during evidentiary hearings, the judge decides admissibility of tests that were challenged by the defense for cause. Evidentiary hearings are part of the criminal court process, discussed in Chapter 5.

CHAPTER ENDNOTES

1. Hamilton v. City of Mesa, 165 Ariz. 513 (Ariz. 1990).

3

Arizona DUI Testing of Blood, Breath, Urine, or Saliva

In the previous chapter we covered field sobriety tests in the DUI case. Now we need to talk about blood, breath, urine, saliva, or other bodily fluid tests used by police to establish the driver's violation of Arizona DUI law.

Alcohol detected in the driver's blood could lead to DUI charges if blood alcohol concentration (BAC) exceeds the legal limit of 0.08%. Prescription drugs, over-the-counter drugs in the driver's body, along with illegal narcotics, designer drugs, and other intoxicating substances, could also result in DUI charges.

From Standard Field Sobriety Tests to Blood Alcohol Concentration

How the driver performed the battery of standard field sobriety tests (SFST), and possibly results from a portable breath test (PBT), could be such that police believe additional tests are warranted to find evidence of driver intoxication or impairment, even if slight.

These tests are intended to produce scientifically accurate, reliable alcohol or drug content levels in the person's bloodstream. Unlike SFST and PBT results, chemical tests are considered to be so scientific, reliable, and accurate that results may be used as evidence of guilt at trial. Not all chemical tests are perfect, of course. Police must have all of their ducks in a row — no errors in test administration, no problems with equipment calibration, no problem with chain of custody, and so on. Defense attorneys routinely challenge chemical tests (breath, blood, urine, saliva, hair) for cause in motions to suppress. When the judge grants the defense' motion to suppress, the test cannot be considered by the fact-finder as proof of guilt at trial.

Blood alcohol concentration in test results can be used to prove that the driver committed a crime. Arizona makes it a crime to drive with certain BAC levels, so breath test or blood test results are strong evidence of a driver's commission of misdemeanor or felony DUI.

Many people are confused by the different tests used in DUI cases. Police are not required to administer SFSTs in every traffic stop before administering a breath test or chemical test. Police have discretion to choose the test or tests they want to administer and will then request them. Consider the driver who exits the vehicle only to fall face first, nose to pavement. The officer would probably skip SFSTs altogether given the driver's condition and request a breath, blood, and chemical test.

The type of test administered is very important. The DUI defense attorney will investigate before the results are used as proof of defendant's guilt. Chemical tests, labs, and law enforcement are not perfect! Mistakes and errors happen, for instance:

- Officer failed to follow standard police procedure in administering test;
- Driver's medical condition render test results unreliable;
- Police failed to properly store test kit prior to use; or
- Indefensible gap in the chain of custody leading up to trial.

There may be defects sufficient to weaken or destroy the state's ability to use chemical test results as evidence of a driver's guilt. Depending upon the circumstances, some tests may be inadmissible at trial against the defendant (for instance, inadmissible evidence because the expiration date had already passed on the test-kit when used on the driver). By comparison, flaws in the test's chain-of-custody generally go to the weight of the evidence (for instance, admissible evidence with less evidentiary weight because there is a lapse in lab documentation).[1]

How do police know which test to give the driver? Generally, it is the law enforcement agency's choice as to which test to give the driver. Police may administer more than one test, too.

Be mindful that, although police have discretion on which test to administer, unless police have a search warrant or there is an exception to the warrant requirement (for example, an open whiskey bottle in plain view), police must first obtain the driver's express consent to testing. If a driver refuses to submit to blood, breath, or chemical test, then police must obtain a warrant before testing may proceed.

How long does it take police to obtain a search warrant to obtain a blood, breath, or other test sample? Phoenix PD, for instance, can expedite a warrant request by filing an **eSearch Warrant** application right from the scene of the police stop. If granted by the judge, in about 10 minutes an electronically signed eSearch Warrant is sent directly to the officer's cruiser. With the search warrant, the test that the driver refused to submit to can be administered by force if necessary. The driver is arrested for DUI, has his or her driver's license revoked for a year for violating the implied consent law, is subject to testing by eSearch Warrant of breath, blood, urine, or other sample as requested by the officer, and may potentially be charged with a DUI misdemeanor or felony.

Why is BAC important to the DUI case? Arizona law criminalizes specific levels of alcohol concentration in a driver's blood. The legal limit in Arizona is BAC 0.08%, meaning a driver's BAC at or above 0.08% violates Arizona DUI law.[2]

However, if the driver is impaired even to the slightest degree, then he or she may still be charged with DUI. That's right, a driver's BAC may be below 0.08% and he or she, if only slightly impaired while operating a motorized vehicle, can be arrested and charged with misdemeanor DUI.

What about driving under the influence of drugs or some other substance? Tests available to police are used to detect other substances as well, such as opioids or marijuana metabolites. A blood sample, particularly, can be used to test for a number of drugs along with accurately determining BAC. Many police officers are also licensed phlebotomists trained to draw blood for test purposes.

Different Types of DUI Tests

We could write volumes on the nuances of each test (some lawyers have), but that's well beyond the scope of this book. Still, the type of test matters a lot in DUI cases. So we'll cover some DUI basics on blood, breath, urine, saliva, and other bodily substance tests.

First, Arizona's DUI statutes link criminality with alcohol concentration in the driver's blood — the BAC level. Upon conviction, defendant's BAC is matched to criminal fines, assessments, and periods of incarceration. Law enforcement typically seek evidence of a driver's BAC by performing a blood test, breath test, or both. Test results are compared to the statute which lists the hierarchy of DUI crime by BAC level. This is proof of intoxication.

To this day, blood testing remains the more accurate method of determining a driver's BAC at or within two hours of arrest. Breath testing is sometimes easier to administer, but BAC results could be slightly less accurate than with blood testing. The driver who is asthmatic, for example, may not be able to exhale enough air to provide an adequate sample for the Intoxilyzer to analyze with any accuracy.

Here is the take away. Every test result offered as evidence of guilt by the state will have numerous vulnerabilities, potential pitfalls, weaknesses, flaws, and ever-present possibility of human error. All test equipment has its requisite calibration. Every test performed must have a provable chain of custody, a diary of what happened to the sample from the moment it was taken to the introduction of test results as evidence in court.

The test-taking procedure, test result, driver's medical circumstances, and other factors all provide opportunity for challenge by the defense. The DUI criminal defense lawyer should be thoroughly versed on each test and be capable of isolating test vulnerabilities under the specific circumstances. Motions to suppress evidence challenge admissibility of BAC and chemical test results.

Driver's Implied Consent to Submit to Blood, Breath, and Other Test

Consent to blood, breath, urine, saliva, or other test is implied simply by obtaining an Arizona driver's license; and by driving within the State of Arizona without regard to domicile or the jurisdiction that issued the driver's license.

> *"A person who operates a motor vehicle in this state gives consent ... to a test or tests of the person's blood, breath, urine or other bodily substance for the purpose of deter-*

> *mining alcohol concentration or drug content if the person is arrested [for DUI] offense ..."*
> *A.R.S. § 28-1321(A).*

A driver placed under arrest for DUI impliedly consents to testing of blood, breath, urine, or other bodily fluid. In that situation, police must have "reasonable grounds to believe" the driver was either under the influence of alcohol or drugs; or the driver was under 21 years of age with "spirituous liquor" in the body. (Arizona is a zero tolerance jurisdiction.)

If the driver was involved in an accident where someone was killed or seriously injured, then he or she impliedly consents to blood, breath, or other testing. In this particular situation, police must have "probable cause to believe that the person caused the accident or the person is issued a [traffic] citation." A.R.S. § 28-673(A).

Implied consent laws are not unique to Arizona. In keeping with Arizona's strict DUI laws, a driver's refusal to submit to testing following a police officer's proper request will result in the immediate surrender of an Arizona driver's license to that officer. Driver's licenses issued by other states cannot be seized in this manner, but driving privileges in Arizona will be suspended. The MVD will suspend driving privileges for at least 12 months. (See Chapter 7 for a discussion about Arizona driver's license suspension and the MVD hearing process.)

If the driver refuses to agree to being tested, then police must contact a judge to obtain a search warrant compelling the driver to submit to testing. Only then can police administer the tests — by force when necessary — to establish BAC or the presence of drugs in the person's body.

Understand that refusing to take the tests will not prevent DUI charges. In situations where the driver violated the implied consent law, the prosecutor frequently cites that refusal as evidence of intoxication. But that's not all.

Here are a few more details on Arizona's implied consent law:

- Standard police procedure requires the officer properly request the test so the driver understands what is being asked and is not effectively forced into submission. For example: If the driver does not speak or read any English, then police should request the test in the driver's language (or police should seek a search warrant).
- Police must properly explain the penalty for violating Arizona's implied consent law so the driver understands the law and can make an informed decision — that is, whether to refuse or recant if there is still time. For example: Instead of blanketly refusing all testing, a

hemophiliac might refuse a blood test, but agree to breathalyzer testing. The diabetic might refuse the breathalyzer, but agree to a blood test. That is because a breath test may show high levels of acetone with diabetes; acetone level being unrelated to BAC.

Even when the driver agrees and submits to the requested test or tests, the arresting officer could still seize the Arizona driver's license, depending upon the circumstances.

Arizona DUI Misdemeanor Offenses

When the driver is charged by the state with DUI, what might those charges be? Most DUIs are misdemeanors, but there are also felony DUIs. Arizona law has four levels of DUI. Each DUI offense has two elements, both of which must be proven beyond a reasonable doubt:

1. Driver had actual physical control of the motor vehicle, and
2. Driver was under the influence of alcohol or drugs.

Take a closer look at both of these elements.

PART I: Actual Physical Control of a Motor Vehicle

What is "actual physical control" of a motor vehicle? This is the driving element of the DUI. Driving requires actual physical control of a vehicle, of course. But what if the driver pulled completely off the road and turned the engine off? In that instance, the driver may or may not be in actual physical control of the vehicle. It depends. The trier of fact determines whether the driver was "simply using the vehicle as a stationary shelter or actually posed a threat to the public by the exercise of present or imminent control over [the vehicle] while impaired" by drugs or alcohol. If the latter, then the driver had actual physical control.[3]

The driver who seemingly did the right thing by pulling off the road, turning off the ignition, and falling asleep may still be in "actual physical control" if it can be inferred by other circumstances that he or she drove the vehicle while impaired.

What if police told the driver to move the car? Absent some other consideration, the driver exercised actual physical control of the car in complying with the officer's request.[4]

PART II: Under the Influence of Alcohol or Drugs

Was the driver under the influence of alcohol or drugs such that a crime was committed? The answer to that question lies in two key misdemeanor DUI statutes — A.R.S. § 28-1381 and A.R.S. § 28-1382. The first statute includes four DUIs described as Section 1, Section 2, Section 3, and Section 4 offenses.

Section 1 DUI: Impaired to the Slightest Degree (BAC Under 0.08%)

In Arizona, it is unlawful to drive or be in actual physical control of a vehicle:

> *"(A)(1). While under the influence of intoxicating liquor, any drug, a vapor releasing substance containing a toxic substance or any combination of liquor, drugs or vapor releasing substances if the person is impaired to the slightest degree."*
>
> *A.R.S. § 28-1381(A)(1).*

Was the driver "under the influence" and "impaired" at time of driving? Driving or being in actual physical control of a motor vehicle while impaired to the slightest degree is a Section 1 DUI. The person under some functional impairment because alcohol or drugs negatively impact his or her judgment or physical coordination could be charged with this Class 1 Misdemeanor. (An affirmative defense to a Section 3 DUI charge may be inapplicable to a Section 1 DUI, as seen later.)

Section 2 DUI: DUI Per Se (0.08% BAC and Higher)

In Arizona, it is unlawful to drive or be in actual physical control of a vehicle:

> *"(A)(2). If the person has an alcohol concentration of 0.08 or more within two hours of driving or being in actual physical control of the vehicle and the alcohol concentration results from alcohol consumed either before or while driving or being in actual physical control of the vehicle."*
>
> *A.R.S. § 28-1381(A)(2).*

To drive or be in actual physical control of a vehicle with a BAC of 0.08% is a Section 2 DUI offense. Note that Section 2 makes no mention of impairment. If the driver's BAC is 0.08% or higher within two hours of driving, then it is a DUI per se. The person is strictly liable for this Class 1 Misdemeanor. No proof of intoxication or impairment while driving is required!

Section 2 adds a two-hour test window for measuring a driver's BAC. Needless to say, law enforcement officers are very motivated to obtain physical evidence (blood, breath, urine, or saliva) within two hours of the traffic stop. This two-hour window is also in Arizona's extreme DUI statute.

When events do not unfold that way for police and more than 120 minutes elapse before testing, evidentiary hurdles toughen for the state. An expert witness must provide relation-back testimony using retroactive extrapolation (retrograde extrapolation) based upon the delayed BAC test.[5] This is to establish what the driver's BAC would have been if blood, breath, or other test had been administered within two hours of driving.

Timing is everything, especially when the unique evidentiary circumstances found in DUI arrests are considered. In other words, most drivers start sobering up in two hours time and BAC levels drop.

How long does it take to sober up? Although much depends upon the individual's physiology (weight, sex, age, health, and so on), in general, BAC levels drop fairly quickly after alcohol intake ceases. As a rule of thumb, one standard drink takes an average person weighing 150 pounds about one hour to metabolize. (This does not apply to drugs!) If the average person consumed four standard drinks in one hour, then it would take at least four hours for the body to metabolize the alcohol.

A standard drink has 0.6 (14 grams) of pure alcohol, but how does beer compare to red wine, or to tequila? The following chart compares alcoholic beverages to establish the standard drink.

What Is One Standard Drink?

Section 3 DUI: Dangerous Drug or Metabolite

In Arizona, it is unlawful to drive or be in actual physical control of a vehicle:

> *"(A)(3). While there is any drug defined in § 13-3401 or its metabolite in the person's body."*
>
> *A.R.S. § 28-1381(A)(2).*

The Section 3 DUI is drugged driving. It is a misdemeanor to drive while under the influence of what are considered to be dangerous drugs, narcotics, or other chemical substances specified in Arizona law. Drug DUIs stem from illegal or illicit drugs found in the person's body, typically after a blood test, as well as legal but dangerous drugs. Dangerous drugs are listed in A.R.S. § 13-3401(6) and include hydrocodone, methamphetamine, mescaline, and many more. Metabolites are chemical by-products of a drug, of which many are uniquely identifiable.

Understand that this is a strict liability offense and a Class 1 Misdemeanor. If the driver had dangerous or narcotic drugs or had drug metabolites capable of causing impairment in his or her body (detected by chemical testing urine or blood, for instance), then drug test evidence is sufficient to support a Section 3 DUI. The prosecutor does not need to prove any driver impairment!

What about prescription drugs and medical marijuana? Valid prescriptions for medical marijuana and narcotics, oxycontin for example, are sometimes a defense to DUI, depending upon the offense charged:

> ***Yes:*** A valid prescription taken at a therapeutic dose by the patient may be a Section 3 DUI defense.
>
> ***No:*** A valid prescription taken at a therapeutic dose by the patient may not be a defense to Section 1 DUI if the driver was impaired in the slightest degree.

Many people have medical marijuana prescriptions for their cancer, chronic pain, and seizure disorders, among other things. However, Arizona DUI law prohibits a person from driving while under the influence of marijuana (cannabis) if impaired,[6] regardless of whether the person had a valid medical marijuana card. As an aside, medical marijuana patients may only legally possess the drug in small amounts. Anything over 2.5 ounces leaves the driver open to a drug possession charge.

With a drug DUI involving medical marijuana, police cannot rely on marijuana metabolites in the driver's body as evidence of DUI. To detect recent marijuana use after an automobile accident, for example, a urine, blood, or saliva test may be administered to detect the existence of marijuana metabolites, but the test cannot be used as proof of driver impairment.

Although some marijuana metabolites are eliminated from the body within a few hours of ingestion, others may linger in the body for weeks depending upon the person's marijuana consumption routine. As a result, there is a high likelihood that any patient using prescription marijuana will test positive for marijuana metabolites, impaired or not.

The Arizona Supreme Court has ruled on the marijuana metabolite question in two DUI cases, both favorable to the defense:

State v. Harris (2014): A patient using prescription marijuana cannot be prosecuted for DUI based solely upon evidence of marijuana metabolites in the body. State v. Harris, 234 Ariz. 343 (2014).

Dobson v. McClennen (2015): A medical marijuana patient may assert a valid prescription as an affirmative defense to DUI. Dobson v. McClennen, No. CV-14-0313-PR, 2015 WL 7353847 (Ariz. Nov. 20, 2015), unanimous. However, a marijuana card does not provide the patient immunity from DUI if, indeed, the driver was impaired. The burden is on the driver to show that the level of marijuana or marijuana metabolites in his or her body was not sufficient to cause impairment to the slightest degree.

Lastly, there is the Section 4 DUI, as follows.

Section 4 DUI: Licensed Commercial Drivers (0.04% BAC and Higher)

In Arizona, it is unlawful for anyone with a commercial driver's license (CDL) to drive or be in actual physical control of a vehicle:

> *"(A)(4). If the vehicle is a commercial motor vehicle that requires a person to obtain a commercial driver license as defined in § 28-3001 and the person has an alcohol concentration of 0.04 or more."*
>
> *A.R.S. § 28-1381(A)(4).*

An individual with a CDL whose breath or blood test is 0.04% BAC or higher will face harsh penalties if convicted of a Section 4 DUI offense, such that his or her CDL could be jeopardized. With a Section 4 conviction, the driver will be prohibited from driving a commercial vehicle for 12 months. It's the same penalty if that driver was convicted of a Section 1, 2, or 3 DUI offense, or violated the implied consent law, while driving a non-commercial vehicle. Often truckers, these drivers are held to a higher standard than regular drivers because of the commercial activities they are routinely involved in.

If your CDL is at risk, consult a DUI defense lawyer with experience handling cases involving commercial drivers. Do not take unnecessary chances with your livelihood if you are a commercial driver!

Extreme DUI in Arizona

The second key Arizona statute is extreme DUI – A.R.S. § 28-1382 – which increases penalties with heightened BAC levels within two hours of driving.

Extreme DUI: 0.15% BAC and Higher

In Arizona, it is unlawful to drive or be in actual physical control of a vehicle if, within two hours of driving, the person:

1. Had a BAC of 0.15% or more, but less than 0.20%; or
2. Had a BAC of 0.20% or higher (sometimes called super-extreme DUI).

Comparing a Section 2 per se DUI violation (A.R.S.§ 28-1381(A)(2)) to an extreme DUI (A.R.S. § 28-1382), the penalties differ, but the same evidentiary issues apply to both. It's a matter of degree. Both Section 2 and extreme DUIs are Class 1 Misdemeanors, too.

What happens with a second DUI conviction? Be mindful that repeat DUI offenders, even on a second DUI offense, face harsher penalties, increased criminal fines and assessments, longer jail sentences, longer suspension of drivers licenses, more community restitution, longer use of ignition interlock devices, and so on. Importantly, after two DUI convictions, a third drunk driving arrest could result in an aggravated DUI charge which is a felony.

Aggravated DUI Felonies in Arizona

In Arizona criminal law, there are four different aggravated DUI felonies:

- **Class 4 Felony:** DUI on suspended, canceled, revoked, refused, or restricted license. A.R.S. § 28-1383(A)(1).
- **Class 4 Felony:** DUI with two prior DUI convictions in past 7 years. A.R.S. § 28-1383(A)(2).
- **Class 4 Felony:** DUI while driver is required to equip any motor vehicle he or she operates with an IID; or refused BAC testing when required to have an IID. A.R.S. § 28-1383(A)(4).
- **Class 6 Felony:** DUI with a child under 15 years of age in the vehicle. A.R.S. § 28-1383(A)(3).

What follows is a brief overview of each DUI felony offense.

Aggravated DUI for Driving on Suspended, Canceled, Revoked, Refused, or Restricted License

Any DUI that occurred while the person was driving under a suspended, canceled, revoked, refused, or restricted license is an aggravated DUI — that's a Class 4 Felony. If the driver was required to equip the vehicle with a certified ignition interlock device (IID), then it's also felony DUI. A.R.S. § 28-1383(A)(4).

Suspended driving privileges need not have been the result of a prior DUI conviction! If the license was suspended, for example, by the MVD for some other traffic violation and the person is later arrested for DUI, then the offense escalates to aggravated DUI.

The same law applies if a license issued by another state, Colorado for example, was suspended, cancelled, restricted, refused, or revoked.

Aggravated DUI with 2 Prior DUI Offenses in 84 Months

Aggravated DUI includes a third DUI conviction within 84 months (seven years). The prior DUI convictions may have been misdemeanors or felonies and are generally proven with documentary evidence (for example, certified copies of two previous DUI convictions). Thereafter, an additional DUI is a Class 4 Felony.

Were priors in another state? If a prior conviction in another state would have been a DUI in Arizona, then a third DUI within seven years is still aggravated DUI.

Aggravated DUI with Child in the Vehicle

Lastly, it is a Class 6 Felony if the DUI occurred while a child under the age of 15 was also in the vehicle.

CHAPTER ENDNOTES

1. State v. Secord, 207 Ariz. 517 (Ariz. Ct. App. 2004).

2. For CDL drivers, the BAC limit is 0.04%. A.R.S. § 28-1381(A)(4). Arizona is zero tolerance for under-aged drivers so a BAC above 0.00% violates DUI law. A.R.S. § 4-244. Few exceptions apply.

3. State v. Love, 182 Ariz. 324 (1995).

4. State v. Tyszkiewicz, 209 Ariz. 457 (Ariz. Ct. App. 2005).

5. State v. Stanley, 217 Ariz. 253 (Ariz. Ct. App. 2007), citing State v. Claybrook, 193 Ariz. 588 (Ariz. Ct. App. 1998).

6. A.R.S. § 28-1381(A)(1).

4

Driver Arrested and Vehicle Impounded

We mentioned earlier that there are many consequences associated with DUI arrest. One of those consequences is vehicle impoundment which, for most people, is more than mere inconvenience. That's especially so when the driver owns the seized vehicle now sitting in a police storage lot somewhere. An impounded vehicle necessary for employment could result in job loss.

With the driver under DUI arrest, police need to get the vehicle removed. But not every vehicle will be impounded. When the driver's spouse is a passenger in the vehicle, then he or she may be allowed to take the keys and drive on home or to a safe place. There are two requirements for that to happen. First, the spouse must have a valid driver's license. Second, police must have reasonable grounds to believe said spouse is not under the influence or impaired, too (or if under the age of 21, the spouse has zero BAC). If there is no one to drive the vehicle, then police will impound it.

How long will the vehicle be impounded after DUI arrest? The vehicle may be impounded for up to 30 days. Impoundment is independent of any DUI charge filed against the driver later. Immobilizing or impounding the vehicle is a penalty related to DUI arrest, but is not dependent upon a DUI charge or conviction. A.R.S. § 28-3511.

Impoundment in many DUI situations is mandatory, including those where the driver:

1. Had a suspended or revoked driver's license, or never had a valid license from any jurisdiction;
2. Was driving with an alien passenger illegally present in the U.S.;
3. Is under age 21 and had any alcohol in the body;
4. Was required to have an ignition interlock device (IID) in the vehicle; or
5. Was arrested for extreme DUI (at or above 0.15% BAC) or aggravated felony DUI.

The vehicle is impounded whether the driver owns it or not. Frequently, the driver is not a registered owner, but is a friend or family member other than the spouse.

The registered owner of the vehicle (or owner's spouse) can get the vehicle out of the tow yard by paying all of the fees and costs. If a hearing request is filed within 10 days, then the owner or owner's spouse may seek early release of the vehicle from the impound agency. Say, for example, the car was stolen and the theft was reported. The registered owner should certainly be able to recover the car from impound early. By contrast, if the vehicle was not stolen, but the registered owner allowed someone to drive it without a valid driver's license, then the owner may be ineligible for early release of his or her vehicle. A.R.S. § 28-3512.

Are there impound charges? Yes. Getting a vehicle out of impound requires payment of all immobilization, towing and storage fees, and administrative fee (unless the vehicle was stolen with the theft reported to law enforcement). When the registered owner or owner's spouse does not claim the vehicle after the 30-day impound period, the unclaimed vehicle is considered abandoned. The impound agency in possession of the vehicle files an abandoned vehicle report. This requires a release for the registered owner to retake possession of his or her vehicle from the impound agency. A.R.S. § 28-3515.

Could the vehicle be forfeited so the driver-owner never gets it back? Yes, that is a possibility. But only in those limited circumstances where the driver was convicted of felony aggravated DUI and was also the vehicle owner. A.R.S. § 28-1384. Forfeited vehicles are sold at police auction and proceeds of the sale are deposited in the state's general fund. An exception to forfeiture may apply. Consult an experienced DUI defense lawyer right away.

Booking By Law Enforcement Following Driver's Arrest

As seen on TV, arrest is followed by booking which is processing at the police station or county sheriff's office. While booking the driver, law enforcement will take mugshots and fingerprints, record identifying marks and tattoos, record personal data (full name, date of birth, physical characteristics like tattoos), and assign a case number.

The general public can access general booking information on police websites. For example, the Maricopa County Sheriff's Office routinely posts mugshots, personal data (name and DOB), and the reason for arrest. Booking information is posted online for several reasons: Community awareness, public notice, and deterrence (general and specific). Following a dismissal of DUI charges or not guilty verdict, mugshots and information should immediately be removed from law enforcement websites.

After booking, especially if this is a first offense, the person is typically released having posted bond or "own recognizance" release with a promise to appear for upcoming court proceedings. If not released, then the person remains in police custody at the city or county jail until arraigned. That's the beginning of criminal court proceedings, the subject of our next chapter.

5
DUI Court Proceedings

Now that the person has been arrested and booked, what happens next? This is where we begin discussing court proceedings. And a lot can happen. To make this part of the criminal process a bit more manageable, we divided DUI criminal proceedings into two chapters. Chapter 5 provides an overview of the court process with explanations about each proceeding. Then Chapter 6 explains the DUI trial in five steps.

Before getting started, understand that there is a big difference between civil and criminal court proceedings. When reading about criminal court proceedings, be mindful of the role our U.S. and state constitutions play in requiring that every defendant be treated fairly throughout the entire process.

A person charged with DUI has important rights under the Due Process Clause of the Fifth Amendment, U.S. Constitution (applied to the states through the Fourteenth Amendment), as well as the Due Process Clause in Article II, Section 4, Arizona Constitution as stated here:

> *"No person shall be deprived of life, liberty, or property without due process of law."*

Due process requires fundamental fairness — substantively and procedurally — before trial, during trial, in sentencing if convicted, and in any appeal that may follow.

Before deciding whether to charge a suspect with misdemeanor DUI or felony DUI (aggravated DUI), the prosecutor can have police continue their investigation post-arrest. Why? To uncover any prior DUI crimes from other jurisdictions which can be added to the police report. Do not be fooled into thinking the DUI case is scratched simply because charges have not yet been filed. If anything, delayed charges can be a red flag warning to take defensive action now. Defensive action includes consulting a DUI defense attorney about pre-charge representation.

Arizona Criminal Procedures in Felony and Misdemeanor DUI Cases

The proceedings for felony aggravated DUI differ somewhat from misdemeanor proceedings. Use the chart below to compare, step-by-step, the criminal court proceedings necessary for felony DUI and misdemeanor DUI.

FELONY DUI	MISDEMEANOR DUI
COURT JURISDICTION: Superior Court has jurisdiction over felony DUI cases.	COURT JURISDICTION: City court (municipal court) has jurisdiction over misdemeanor DUI cases within the city limits. If the DUI arrest was outside the city limits, then the county Justice Court has jurisdiction to hear the case. Aggravated DUI charges (felonies) must be filed in Superior Court.
FELONY CHARGE: A felony aggravated DUI charge can come from the county attorney by complaint (or "information") or by Grand Jury indictment. A felony charge must be supported by a finding of probable cause. CHARGE BY COMPLAINT: If the charge comes directly from the county attorney, then there is a preliminary hearing (see below) at which the judge determines whether there is probable cause. Probable cause means enough evidence shows that a crime was committed and that the suspect should stand trial on the allegations. CHARGE BY INDICTMENT: 15 jurors make up	MISDEMEANOR CHARGE: The city attorney or county attorney brings a misdemeanor DUI complaint against the suspect. City attorneys do not handle felony cases.

FELONY DUI	MISDEMEANOR DUI
a standard Grand Jury. If at least 9 jurors find probable cause, then they indict. Only the prosecutor presents evidence to the Grand Jury. DISMISSED: If there is no finding of probable cause, then the case must be dismissed. FILED: If probable cause is found, then felony DUI charges are filed with the Superior Court.	
INITIAL APPEARANCE: The initial appearance hearing is held within 24 hours of arrest when the suspect is still in police custody. When the suspect was released after arrest, the hearing notice and summons are sent to the person's address. At this hearing, the suspect appears before the court for the first time and is informed of the felony DUI charge against him or her by information or indictment. The court informs defendant of the right to attorney representation. If the court finds that defendant cannot afford an attorney, then an attorney will be appointed from the Public Defender's Office. The court establishes the conditions of the defendant's release (bail bond or on own recognizance). The court may order the defendant remain jailed without bail to protect community safety. The court then sets the date for the next proceeding in felony prosecution – the preliminary hearing. NOTE: With Grand Jury indictment, defendant's arraignment (below) may immediately follow the initial appearance.	INITIAL APPEARANCE: Generally, this does not happen in a misdemeanor DUI unless you were arrested and booked into jail. This process would be similar to the felony process.

FELONY DUI	MISDEMEANOR DUI
PRELIMINARY HEARING: This is a probable cause hearing in open court following the county attorney's direct complaint against defendant alleging felony DUI. To establish probable cause, the prosecutor presents evidence and witnesses showing a felony crime was committed and that the suspect should stand trial for the allegations. The DUI criminal defense attorney may cross-examine the arresting officer (the state's witness) and may present witnesses, too. DISMISSED: If the court does not find probable cause, then the case is dismissed. CHARGED: If the court finds probable cause, then the suspect is arraigned.	Not applicable to misdemeanor DUI.
FELONY ARRAIGNMENT: The defendant makes a brief appearance at the Superior Court arraignment to be informed of the felony DUI charges against him or her, and upon which the court or Grand Jury has determined probable cause. When defendant is arraigned, he or she appears and enters a plea to the charges: "Guilty" or "Not Guilty" (a "No Contest" plea is treated as "Guilty"). If defendant refuses to plead, then a "Not Guilty" plea is entered. GUILTY PLEA: There is no trial because defendant admitted guilt. The case is scheduled for sentencing. NOT GUILTY PLEA: Criminal trial is scheduled. NO CONTEST PLEA: Sentencing is scheduled. The court then sets the date for the next proceeding in the felony prosecution – the pre-trial conference.	**MISDEMEANOR ARRAIGNMENT:** After the prosecutor files a misdemeanor DUI complaint, the defendant appears in Municipal Court or Justice Court to enter a plea of "Guilty" or "Not Guilty" (a "No Contest" plea is treated as "Guilty"). If defendant refuses to plead, then a "Not Guilty" plea is entered. The defendant represented by a DUI defense attorney can have the attorney waive arraignment and enter a Not Guilty plea. Once the court is notified of attorney representation, it sends all notices of hearing dates to defendant's lawyer. GUILTY PLEA: There is no trial because defendant has admitted guilt. Sentencing usually happens immediately. NOT GUILTY PLEA: Criminal trial is scheduled. NO CONTEST PLEA: There is no trial because defendant has admitted guilt. Sentencing usually happens immediately.

FELONY DUI	MISDEMEANOR DUI
	The court sets the date for the next proceeding in misdemeanor prosecution – the pre-trial conference.
PRE-TRIAL CONFERENCE: This conference with prosecutor, defense attorney, and judge is where the attorneys apprise the court on the status of the felony case. Is the case resolved? Are plea negotiations continuing? Is the DUI defense lawyer's investigation ongoing? The court is informed of outstanding legal issues it will need resolved. Though there are outstanding legal issues, the case may be set for trial. That a trial is scheduled does not mean that trial is certain.	PRE-TRIAL CONFERENCE: The prosecutor and defense attorney conference to discuss the case and inform the judge on the status. Is the case resolved? Are plea negotiations continuing? Is the DUI defense lawyer's investigation ongoing? The court is informed of outstanding legal issues it will need resolved. Though outstanding legal issues remain, the case may be set for trial. That a trial is scheduled does not mean that trial is certain.
EVIDENTIARY HEARINGS AND ORAL ARGUMENT ON PRE-TRIAL MOTIONS: In a felony case, the judge decides issues of law and the jury decides issues of fact. Admissibility of evidence is a question of law for the judge to decide. Using pre-trial motions, both attorneys ask the judge to decide specific issues of law. For instance, admissibility of evidence (such as a chemical test) is a question of law for the judge to decide. If a hearing is requested and scheduled on a pre-trial motion, then defense attorney and prosecutor can each present oral argument on how the judge should rule on the motion. Testimony at the hearing may assist the judge in ruling on the motion.	EVIDENTIARY HEARINGS AND ORAL ARGUMENT ON PRE-TRIAL MOTIONS: A misdemeanor DUI trial could be a bench or a jury trial. With a bench trial, the judge decides issues of law and issues of fact. With a jury trial, the judge decides issues of law and the jury decides issues of fact. Using pre-trial motions, both attorneys ask the judge to decide certain issues of law. For instance, admissibility of evidence (such as witness testimony) is a question of law for the judge to decide, not the jury. If a hearing is requested and scheduled on a pre-trial motion, then defense attorney and prosecutor can each present oral argument on how the judge should rule on the motion. Testimony at the hearing may assist the judge in ruling on the motion.

FELONY DUI

PRE-TRIAL MANAGEMENT CONFERENCE:

Scheduling a pre-trial management conference presumes trial is imminent. The conference is an opportunity for the prosecutor and defense attorney to ask the judge to resolve any outstanding questions of law. Typically there is a week or more between the management conference and the trial date and, during the interim, charges could be dismissed or a plea deal could be reached.

FELONY DUI TRIAL:

Defendant is entitled to a trial by jury with a felony DUI. The jury decides questions of fact; the judge decides questions of law. (Only rarely will there be a bench trial in a felony case.)

Whether the prosecutor proved every element of the DUI crime "beyond a reasonable doubt" is a question of fact for the jury. If YES, then defendant is Guilty. If NO, then defendant is Not Guilty.

The jury in a felony DUI trial must be made up of 8 to 12 jurors. The jury's verdict must be unanimous. If the jury is not unanimous, then it cannot render a verdict and the judge must declare mistrial. Because there is no verdict in a mistrial, the court sets a new trial. This is not a constitutional violation of the double jeopardy clause.

JURY'S GUILTY VERDICT: The unanimous jury convicts the defendant with a Guilty verdict. The defendant may be taken into custody.

JURY'S NOT GUILTY VERDICT: The unanimous jury finds the defendant Not Guilty which

MISDEMEANOR DUI

PRE-TRIAL MANAGEMENT CONFERENCE:

In a misdemeanor criminal case, a pre-trial management conference is not always necessary. But if the conference is scheduled, the prosecutor and defense attorney will have another opportunity to present any lingering questions of law to the judge before trial begins.

Typically there is a week or more between the management conference and trial date which, during the interim, means the charges could still be dismissed or a plea deal could be reached.

MISDEMEANOR DUI TRIAL:

Because defendant is entitled to a trial by jury, there are two possibilities with misdemeanor DUI. Either the defendant does not request jury trial and a bench trial commences with judge deciding both questions of law and questions of fact. Or the defendant requests a jury trial with the judge deciding questions of law and jury deciding questions of fact.

Whether the prosecutor proved every element of the DUI crime "beyond a reasonable doubt" is a question of fact. If YES, then defendant is Guilty. If NO, then defendant is Not Guilty.

The jury in a misdemeanor DUI trial must be made up of at least 6 jurors. The jury's verdict must be unanimous. If the jury is not unanimous, then it cannot render a verdict and the judge declares a mistrial. Because there is no verdict in a mistrial, the court sets a new trial. This is not a constitutional violation of the double jeopardy clause.

JUDGE'S GUILTY VERDICT: In a bench trial, the judge finds the defendant Guilty as charged and convicts.

FELONY DUI	MISDEMEANOR DUI
results in the person's immediate release. MISTRIAL: No jury unanimity means no verdict. The judge declares a mistrial and orders a new trial. If the defendant is found Guilty of aggravated DUI, then a sentencing hearing is set.	JUDGE'S NOT GUILTY VERDICT: In a bench trial, the judge finds the defendant Not Guilty as charged and the person is immediately released. - OR - JURY'S GUILTY VERDICT: In a jury trial, the unanimous jury convicts the defendant with a Guilty verdict. JURY'S NOT GUILTY VERDICT: In a jury trial, the unanimous jury finds the defendant Not Guilty which results in the person's immediate release. MISTRIAL: In a jury trial, no unanimity means no verdict. The judge declares a mistrial and orders a new trial. If the defendant is found Guilty of misdemeanor DUI, then the judge will sentence the individual at a sentencing hearing held after the verdict. Or the judge may set a sentencing hearing for later.
FELONY AGGRAVATED DUI SENTENCING: The defendant found Guilty by trial verdict or plea agreement will be sentenced to punishment. The sentencing hearing will be scheduled about 30 days after the trial finding of guilt or after the approved plea agreement. PRE-SENTENCE REPORT: In preparation for sentencing, a probation officer meets with the defendant, prepares a pre-sentence report, and submits the report to the sentencing judge with recommendations. Defense and prosecution are present at the sentencing hearing. Each can provide input and evidence to assist the judge in deciding an appropriate sentence for this defendant.	MISDEMEANOR DUI SENTENCING: The defendant found Guilty by trial verdict or plea agreement will be sentenced to punishment. The sentencing hearing in a misdemeanor case typically follows on the same day as the finding of defendant's guilt. Defense and prosecution are present at the sentencing hearing. Each can provide input and evidence to assist the judge in deciding on an appropriate sentence for this defendant. Victims may also address the court at the sentencing hearing. SENTENCE ORDER: This is the judge's order on the sentence the defendant shall serve as punishment.

FELONY DUI	MISDEMEANOR DUI
Victims may also address the court at the sentencing hearing. SENTENCE ORDER: This is the judge's order on the sentence the defendant shall serve as punishment.	
PUNISHMENT: The sentence order is imposed on the convicted felon.	PUNISHMENT: The sentence order is imposed on the convicted misdemeanant.
APPEAL: The convicted defendant has a limited time to file a Notice of Appeal.	APPEAL: The convicted defendant has a limited time to file a Notice of Appeal.

NOTES:

Negotiating a Plea Bargain in Arizona DUI Cases

In almost every DUI case, the defendant has an opportunity to negotiate a deal with the prosecutor. Plea bargaining is a much misunderstood and often maligned process.

Many DUI cases are resolved before trial. But if not, then the defense and prosecution enter into final plea negotiations. Before considering any plea offer, all discovery of evidence relevant to defendant's case should be complete!

When the prosecutor makes a plea offer, the defendant either accepts the offer or rejects it. If rejected, then the DUI case proceeds to trial. Proceeding with a criminal trial means the accused wishes to fight the state's allegations.

What is plea bargaining? Plea negotiations between the state and the defense may include a plea deal that charges a defendant with a lesser offense. The prosecutor may offer a lesser penalty for the offense charged. The prosecutor may drop some, possibly most, of the charges against the defendant. The prosecutor may offer alternative sentencing and will support that sentencing strategy with the judge.

Some DUI cases settle before the pre-trial conference

is even held. If the case is not resolved through negotiations, then a trial may be set. Understand that just because the judge schedules a trial does not make it a certainty. Much can happen between this point in the proceedings and the trial date.

What are the possible results of plea bargaining? There are several possibilities:

- Settlement (plea deal)
- Dismissal of some charges
- Dismissal of the worst charge
- Reduced sentence
- Probation
- Drug or alcohol treatment program (AA or other detox program)
- Residential treatment center (live-in)
- Electronic home monitoring (ankle bracelets)
- Counseling
- Work program on weekends
- Community service (restitution)

A plea agreement means defendant pleads Guilty and will be convicted. Not every defendant accepts a plea deal and conviction. A plea agreement requires admission of guilt, with the main points negotiated being "guilty of what?" followed by "with what punishment?"

Before any plea agreement is binding, the judge must approve it. If a plea agreement includes probation, a violation of the terms of probation can result in jail time. To remain free from custody to be with family, keep a job, and live a normal life, the defendant must comply with **all** terms of the plea agreement or terms of sentencing. In addition to incarceration, violating any condition of probation or sentencing could eliminate any possibility of setting aside the judgment of guilt later on. This means:

- Do pay all fines and assessments;
- Do complete all counseling sessions;
- Do complete all drug and alcohol screenings;
- Do comply with all of the judge's sentencing terms; and
- Do Not commit any new crime.

Following any criminal conviction, store the plea agreement (if there is one) and sentencing documents in a secure place for safekeeping. A criminal conviction remains on one's record so sentencing documents are very important papers. Hold on to them. At some point it may be possible to petition to have the judgment set aside.

What is setting aside the judgment of guilt? Under Arizona law, a person convicted of a DUI has the right to petition the court in the future to have the judgment of guilt set aside (similar to expungement). Set aside cleans up a criminal record, but does not erase it.

When the request is granted, the judge's set aside order dismisses all charges and releases the individual from all penalties and disabilities connected with the conviction. This can be very beneficial for the individual and his or her family.

A felony or misdemeanor set aside, however, does not make the conviction disappear from one's criminal record. Instead, the record is updated to include the court's set aside order confirming that the person completed every condition of probation or sentencing, that the conviction was **vacated**, and that the charges were **dismissed**. Needless to say, no court will consider hearing a petition for set aside until after all conditions of probation and sentencing have been fully complied with.

Because a petition to set aside the judgment of guilt is typically a long way off, it is a good idea make arrangements to contact the criminal defense attorney when all conditions of probation or sentencing have been met.

6

DUI Trial in 5 Steps

Throughout this book, we have touched on different aspects of the criminal trial. Now it's time to focus on **five steps in the DUI trial process** starting with defendant's constitutional right to a trial by jury.

The discussion that follows is very general, but the steps will apply to both aggravated DUI (felony trial) and misdemeanor DUI (misdemeanor trial). For more details about a particular phase of the trial, such as jury selection or breath test expert witness testimony, consult an experienced DUI defense lawyer.

Step 1: Jury Trial or Bench Trial

Bench Trial: There is no jury in a bench trial. With a bench trial, the judge is the sole fact-finder and decides all matters of law and criminal procedure. The defendant has a constitutional right to trial by jury. But if the defendant does not want a jury trial, then there will be a bench trial.

Jury Trial: In a jury trial, the jurors are the finders of fact while the judge decides all matters of law and criminal procedure. The jury must be empanelled which involves jury selection and voir dire. Not every criminal trial must have 12 jurors, although many do. There may be only eight jurors in an Arizona felony DUI trial, but never fewer. There must be at least six jurors in a misdemeanor DUI trial.

Any jury verdict of "Guilty" or "Not Guilty" must be unanimous. If not, then there is a mistrial. Where there is no unanimity, there is no verdict — often called the "hung jury." When the jury is undecided, the judge declares a mistrial and sets the case for a new trial. With a new trial, a new jury is empanelled. For the defendant, a mistrial could mean plea negotiations are resumed (motivated by the prosecutor's desire to avoid more time, expense, and uncertainty of another trial). A new trial does not violate the double jeopardy clause.

Whether bench trial or jury trial, the defendant is

present for the court proceedings.

Step 2: Presenting the Case

Opening Statements: Both prosecutor and defense attorney make opening statements. Because the burden of proof is on the state, the prosecutor goes first. The defense attorney may delay giving an opening statement until after close of the state's case.

Burden of Proof: The burden of proof is beyond a reasonable doubt in a criminal case. That burden of proof is on the state. The prosecutor must prove every element of the DUI crime beyond a reasonable doubt to obtain a conviction. Anything less and the defendant cannot be convicted of the crime.

State Presents Its Case: The prosecutor presents the state's evidence. This includes testimony from the arresting officer as the prosecutor's key witness. At close of the state's case, the defense may motion to dismiss for lack of evidence sufficient for DUI conviction. Then the state rests its case.

Before moving on to the next general step in the DUI trial, there are a few things to know about police testimony.

What the arresting officer witnessed during the traffic stop is crucial to the state's DUI case against the driver. At a police stop, the officer begins preparing a police report, documenting everything observed from the moment he or she begins approaching the subject's vehicle. The officer will be a witness for the state and testifies at trial and at the MVD hearing (assuming there is one).

The defense attorney interviews the officer during the pre-trial phase of the criminal court proceedings. The interview typically takes place at the police station or some other mutually acceptable location. The officer must reasonably cooperate with defense counsel in scheduling the interview, or deposition.

As an objective observer, everything the officer saw and recorded regarding the driver's physical condition and mental state, including any indicia of intoxication (for example, slurred speech or stumbling upon exiting the car), will be in the police report. The prosecutor can then offer the police report into evidence against the driver through the officer's testimony.

Police do not give medical opinions on whether the driver was intoxicated. However, police may testify about what they saw and that a driver's conduct appeared to be influenced by alcohol or that the driver exhibited signs of being intoxicated.

The officer's observations during the police stop and arrest may be explained away by the defense. Erroneous conclusions are drawn from what is observed. Just because the officer recorded his observations does not mean the conclusions drawn from those observations were correct ones.

That the officer records observations in a police report does not mean the driver did not have some non-DUI related reason for why the driver's speech was slurred (driver is deaf or has a speech impediment) or why the driver stumbled getting out of the car (driver had foot surgery or hypoglycemia). Now back to the trial.

Defense Presents Its Case: If the defense attorney did not give an opening statement, then that's done now. The defense presents its case and puts on its evidence. An expert witness may testify, for instance, about mishandling of the blood test or mis-calibration of the breathalyzer device. Although a defendant has the right to testify at his or her own trial, very rarely is that a good idea. Most defendants do not testify at their own criminal trials. In large part that is because, once the defendant testifies, he or she is subject to cross examination by the prosecutor. Finally, the defense rests its case.

Closing Arguments: After the defense rests, both attorneys present their final, closing arguments. First, the prosecution, then the defense, and, lastly, the prosecution.

Step 3: Verdict

Jury deliberations begin: The jury retires to the jury room and deliberates over the case. The jury decides the verdict. Whether felony or misdemeanor DUI, the unanimous jury finds the defendant Not Guilty or Guilty. If the jury is undecided, then there is a mistrial (hung jury). Mistrial is only possible when a jury lacks unanimity. With a Not Guilty verdict, defendant is immediately released — the person is free to go. With a Guilty verdict, defendant is convicted of the crime charged.

After a Guilty verdict, defense may file a post-trial motion to set aside the verdict because, for instance, the defense believes the verdict went against the great weight of the evidence. This is not an appeal. Instead, the defendant is asking the court to re-examine the evidence presented at trial. Although this motion is rarely granted, if it is granted then it could result in a finding of Not Guilty. In which case, there would be no need to file for an appeal, which is the final step in the criminal trial process.

Step 4: Sentencing

Because the defendant was convicted of DUI by Guilty verdict or convicted after accepting a plea agreement, he or she is sentenced. Sentencing applies the punishment for having been convicted of committing the DUI felony or misdemeanor crime.

With a misdemeanor conviction, sentencing phase typically follows right after the trial. If defendant pleaded Guilty, then sentencing follows immediately thereafter. With a felony conviction, the sentencing hearing is set about 30 days after trial. During that time, the probation department prepares a pre-sentence report containing defendant's information and important recommendations to assist the judge before the sentencing hearing.

Victims' Bill of Rights: This is a good opportunity to mention that a victim of the driver's drunk or impaired driving has rights under the Arizona Constitution. Those rights include being notified of criminal proceedings and being present at many of them, including the sentencing hearing. Not every DUI has a victim, but if someone was injured, killed, or had property damage, then the victim's rights might have an impact. Arizona Constitution, Article 2, Section 2.1 is the Victims' Bill of Rights.

VICTIMS' BILL OF RIGHTS: Arizona Constitution, Article 2, Section 2.1

(A) To preserve and protect victims' rights to justice and due process, a victim of crime has a right:

1. To be treated with fairness, respect, and dignity, and to be free from intimidation, harassment, or abuse, throughout the criminal justice process.
2. To be informed, upon request, when the accused or convicted person is released from custody or has escaped.
3. To be present at and, upon request, to be informed of all criminal proceedings where the defendant has the right to be present.
4. To be heard at any proceeding involving a post-arrest release decision, a negotiated plea, and sentencing.
5. To refuse an interview, deposition, or other discovery request by the defendant, the defendant's attorney, or other person acting on behalf of the defendant.
6. To confer with the prosecution, after the crime against the victim has been charged, before trial or before any disposition of the case and to be informed of the disposition.
7. To read pre-sentence reports relating to the crime against the victim when they are available to the defendant.
8. To receive prompt restitution from the person or persons convicted of the criminal conduct that caused the victim's loss or injury.
9. To be heard at any proceeding when any post-conviction release from confinement is being considered.
10. To a speedy trial or disposition and prompt and final conclusion of the case after the conviction and sentence.
11. To have all rules governing criminal procedure and the admissibility of evidence in all criminal proceedings protect victims' rights and to have these rules be subject to amendment or repeal by the legislature to ensure the protection of these rights.
12. To be informed of victims' constitutional rights.

(B) A victim's exercise of any right granted by this section shall not be grounds for dismissing any criminal proceeding or setting aside any conviction or sentence.

(C) "Victim" means a person against whom the criminal offense has been committed or, if the person is killed or incapacitated, the person's spouse, parent, child or other lawful representative, except if the person is in custody for an offense or is the accused.

(D) The legislature, or the people by initiative or referendum, have the authority to enact substantive and procedural laws to define, implement, preserve and protect the rights guaranteed to victims by this section, including the authority to extend any of these rights to juvenile proceedings.

(E) The enumeration in the constitution of certain rights for victims shall not be construed to deny or disparage others granted by the legislature or retained by victims.

Sentencing Hearing: At a sentencing hearing, the judge applies sentencing guidelines to the DUI conviction. This is not optional, DUIs have mandatory sentences upon conviction. Arizona DUI sentencing is very complicated!

Basically, a presumptive sentence serves as a point of departure with sentence minimums and maximums that cannot be exceeded. From there, the judge considers any mitigating factors (easing punishment) or aggravating factors (toughening punishment); these represent deviations from the presumptive DUI sentence in the guidelines. Deviations can neither be less punishment than the minimum, nor more punishment than the maximum allowed sentence under the guidelines.

Finally, the judge enters the sentencing order. A sentencing order can include an order of confinement specifying the period of time defendant will spend in jail, plus any programs available to that individual. If ordered to self-surrender, defendant must deliver himself or herself to the jail and serve out the sentence ordered by the judge.

There are four confinement possibilities with self-surrender:

- **Work Release:** Released from custody to work at a job, returning to the jail each evening until the sentence is fulfilled.

- **Work Furlough:** Under probation officer supervision, defendant is released from jail for specified hours to work at a job, returning to jail each day (or night) until the sentence is completed.

- **Self-Surrender Flat Time (or Straight Time):** Defendant is confined for a specified period with no release until the full sentence is served.

- **Weekend Self-Surrender:** Sentence is served incrementally, as with consecutive weekends.

When the court's order of confinement allows self-surrender to the jail, failure or refusal to self-surrender at the time required can result in re-arrest.

Step 5: Appeal

Although appeal is not really a part of the trial and has a completely different set of court rules, it's the first thing people need to know about should things go against them at trial or sentencing.

Trials are not always fair. Defendants are not always given sufficient time to plead their case. A plea could be made under duress or without appropriate knowledge. Sentencing is not always deserved or in keeping with the DUI sentencing guidelines. The risk of hiring an inexperienced defense attorney can result in counsel being ineffective or having made a serious error during trial.

In our criminal justice system, appeals go to the Arizona Court of Appeals, then to the Arizona Supreme Court, and then all the way to the U.S. Supreme Court. Rarely does a criminal appeal make it that far, though.

In Arizona criminal appellate procedure, the defendant has a limited amount of time after the trial to file an appeal. Appellate practice is complicated and highly technical. This is something to discuss with a criminal defense lawyer who has a solid background in appellate law and practice. Additionally, criminal appeals can take a long time, even years.

What are some examples of criminal appeals? Importantly, Rule 32 of the Arizona Rules of Criminal Procedure sets forth regulations for post-conviction relief. Grounds for filing the Rule 32 petition include:

- Unconstitutional conviction or sentence;
- No jurisdiction for a specific court to order conviction or sentence; or
- New materials and evidence found after trial with power to change the verdict.

Even the best, most experienced DUI defense

attorney cannot control everything that happens at trial and sentencing. The lawyer's knowledge and experience with criminal appellate practice is something to consider when seeking legal representation.

7

MVD Hearings and Drivers License Suspension

One serious consequence of DUI arrest is suspension of your driver's license by the Motor Vehicle Division (MVD) of the Arizona Department of Transportation (ADOT). Out-of-state drivers arrested for DUI may have their driving privileges in Arizona suspended, too, with additional repercussions possible in their home states.

When someone is arrested for DUI, the arresting officer immediately notifies MVD. The MVD then issues a notice of suspension to the driver at the address on record for having violated Arizona traffic law. Once the Arizona driver's license is suspended, only MVD can reinstate it following application and fees paid.

A DUI arrest does not mean MVD must suspend the driver's license without hearing the driver's side of the story. There are legal options and defenses. One thing is certain, failing to file a timely request for MVD hearing after notice of suspension will result in a suspended driver's license.

MVD Case Is Separate from the Criminal Case

The MVD's actions against the driver's license are separate from DUI criminal charges. Yes, both stem from being arrested for DUI, but MVD can take action to suspend driving privileges before there is any criminal trial or conviction. And if MVD did not suspend driving privileges before a conviction, then it will certainly do so after a DUI conviction.

Will the public defender represent the defendant at an MVD hearing? No. The Public Defender's Office only represents clients in criminal proceedings. MVD is an administrative agency and the proceedings are civil, not criminal. For MVD representation, which is highly recommended, the defendant should hire a private lawyer. Why is this so important? First, because the MVD hearing could impact the criminal prosecution and, second, because a suspended driver's license is a big deal that might be avoidable.

Some people do not challenge MVD on license suspension for a number of reasons, including embarrassment, disbelief, and misunderstanding. But loss of driving privileges for three months, 12 months, maybe 24 months, depending upon the circumstances, is a substantial burden worthy of careful consideration. Along with the many things we take for granted, such as a quick run to the grocery store, a driver's license suspension makes it difficult to find employment, obtain child custody, and travel anywhere. Day-to-day living is far more complicated when driving is forbidden.

MVD Proceedings

How MVD proceeds in suspending driving privileges following DUI arrest begins with two Arizona statutes:

- Admin per se suspension under A.R.S. § 28-1385 requires that police report the DUI arrest to MVD; and
- Implied consent suspension under A.R.S. § 28-1321 is Arizona's implied consent law.

After a DUI arrest, the police officer notifies MVD on whether the driver agreed to or refused blood, breath, urine, or other test. If the driver agreed to submit to testing and no warrant was needed, then MVD admin per se suspension procedure under A.R.S. § 28-1385 follows. However, if the driver refused to submit to testing, then MVD implied consent suspension procedure under A.R.S. § 28-1321 follows. That is so, even if a test was ultimately completed by search warrant. By refusing to agree to a test, the driver may have sealed his or her fate in this regard.

With an admin per se violation (A.R.S. § 28-1385) or implied consent violation (A.R.S. § 28-1321), on MVD mailed Notice of Suspension, the individual has three options:

1. Do nothing (default);
2. Request MVD hearing; or
3. Request MVD summary review.

There is a cost for doing nothing. Essentially, default means the person agrees to the suspension. Taking no action to stop or delay license suspension will result in driving privileges terminating 15 days after the notice of suspension. End of story.

With default to admin per se suspension, after the initial 30 days of the 90-day suspension, the driver may obtain a restricted license from MVD. This allows limited driving for the remaining 60 days of the suspension.

With implied consent suspension, doing nothing means the one-year suspension goes into effect 15 days after MVD mailed the notice of suspension. Again, if the driver refused to agree to testing in another incident within the past five years, then a two-year suspension begins.

Some individuals stipulate to admin per se suspension. When unsure whether to plead Guilty or Not Guilty in the DUI criminal case, or when unsure whether trial will be successful, the defendant might stipulate to the license suspension. Should the suspension be upheld at an MVD hearing — with a first offense and no prior DUI or reckless driving convictions — the person will be eligible for 30/60 suspension (discussed below).

Requesting MVD Hearing

Once served with the notice of suspension, a driver has 15 days from the date the notice was mailed to request an MVD hearing. At the hearing, the person may challenge the license suspension and obtain important police testimony.

Normally, only the Administrative Law Judge (ALJ), arresting officer, breath testing officer (if a breath test case), and private defense attorney are present at the MVD hearing. The prosecutor is not present, which means the defense attorney can ask the arresting officer many questions, ones not normally allowed in criminal proceedings. An experienced defense lawyer knows how to use the arresting officer's testimony at the MVD hearing to best advantage in the criminal proceedings.

The request having been made, two or three months may pass before the MVD hearing date. During the interim, the driver's license is still valid. However, the driver will have a yellow MVD copy (breath case) or an MVD computer entry confirming that the driver is permitted to drive (blood case).

What if the suspension is voided at the MVD hearing, but the defendant is found guilty (or pleads guilty) in the criminal case? The MVD gets "another bite at the apple" and will suspend driving privileges if the defendant entered a Guilty plea or was found Guilty in the criminal case.

With a first DUI conviction, MVD may suspend the license for 90 days. With a second DUI in five years or, alternatively, a first DUI with a prior reckless driving conviction in the last seven years, then MVD will suspend driving privileges for 12 months and require an SR22.

If SR22 insurance coverage is required, then the driver pays a premium to have the insurance company send a status letter to MVD. Should a driver's car insurance lapse for any reason (nonpayment of premiums, for example), then the insurance company notifies both the insured and MVD stating that insurance coverage has lapsed. This violation is quickly followed by MVD suspending the driver's license.

Request for MVD Summary Review

The MVD summary review has limited use, but can be invaluable in certain circumstances. If the officer's DUI report is fatally defective, then summary review can result in the citation being thrown out entirely. No traffic citation, no case.

One possible defect is an officer's failure to include breath BAC level when the citation is for an admin per se violation. With an implied consent violation, a defect occurs when police did not describe or reference the driver's condition. This is "required to establish reasonable grounds to believe that a person was driving under the influence of liquor or drugs." Pearson v. MVD-ADOT, 181 Ariz. 235, 889 P2d 28 (Ariz. App 1995).

The driver can request an MVD hearing or summary review, but not both. Be mindful that the arresting officer may correct the defect and provide only the corrected report to MVD. Although this may seem unfair, on summary review the ALJ will rely on the corrected report provided by police, not the defective prior-version.

If there is any notion that a fatal defect will be cured before summary review, the defense lawyer could provide a separate request for each proceeding asking that, should the defect be cured, the ALJ vacate the request for summary review and substitute it with the hearing request.

Alcohol Screening to Obtain a Work Permit

With a first offense, the person is eligible for 30/60 suspension — total suspension 90 days. With 30/60 suspension, there is absolutely no driving for the first 30 days. For the next 60 days, the person can drive to and from work, school, doctor's appointments, and alcohol treatment with a restricted license, or work permit. To get a work permit for the final 60 days of a 90-day suspension, an alcohol screening must occur during the first 30 days. Do not drive yourself to the screening!

An alcohol screening is an interview with an MVD-approved alcohol/drug screener. Screening is required whether an MVD hearing was requested or not. The screener recommends classes which could start right away or be delayed until after restricted driving privileges are reinstated.

Out-of-state residents must complete alcohol screening, too. For those who live in Nevada, Colorado, or California, for example, out-of-state screening is required and must be Arizona-certified.

Taking the initiative and starting alcohol treatment classes before being required to do so can be beneficial, not just personally, but for the DUI criminal case. Although not required, the judge, prosecutor, or both could factor in defendant's proactive effort in dealing with an alcohol or drug problem. Taking classes early certainly won't hurt and could be beneficial.

Driver's License Reinstatement

Too many people make the mistake of not getting their licenses reinstated after their work permits expire. Reinstatement is not automatic! When the period of suspension ends, the driver must go to MVD to get driving privileges reinstated. Until that's done, the license is suspended.

The person who did not apply for reinstatement and did not pay the reinstatement fee remains on suspended status indefinitely. Another DUI while driving on suspended license is aggravated DUI, a class 4 felony. Remember to go down to MVD and apply to reinstate your driving privileges immediately after the 90-day suspension period ends. Because on day 91, it's back to suspended status!

8

CHECKLIST: Choosing a DUI Criminal Defense Attorney

In previous chapters, we touched on just about every important aspect of the Arizona DUI case, from police stop to license reinstatement. Although we covered a lot of ground, some reader's questions surely remain unanswered. Therefore, it's time to talk about hiring an experienced criminal defense lawyer for representation in all DUI criminal proceedings and, too, the MVD hearing.

Hopefully we have made the case for why legal representation is essential for the best possible outcome. DUI law is uniquely complex — the charges, the evidence, the trial, the sentencing. We have talked generally about DUI law, but nothing takes the place of specific legal advice. And specific legal advice should only come from a qualified attorney licensed to practice law in the State of Arizona.

Before reading through the checklist in this chapter, carefully reflect on your need to hire experienced legal representation. If you don't have the financial resources to pay a private attorney, then do obtain legal representation through the Office of the Public Defender. We strongly advise against attempting to represent yourself in criminal proceedings. Even among criminal defense lawyers, DUI representation is something special. Experience really matters.

Use this handy checklist to hire your lawyer. Make copies, one for every attorney you consider and interview. Having the right attorney for you is an essential component of your defense. This is someone who will be entrusted with very sensitive, personal information. There's not a lot of time, so get started as soon as possible.

If it helps, go ahead and rank the attorneys under consideration with a number from 1 to 5 for every item on the following checklist. 1 being weakest and 5 being strongest.

CHECKLIST OF WHAT TO ASK THE ATTORNEY

- ✓ Do you have substantial experience as a criminal defense lawyer?
- ✓ Is criminal defense representation the main focus of your law practice?
- ✓ What are your credentials? Where did you graduate from law school?
- ✓ Have you been attorney-rated by clients and peers? Are you AV-rated (preeminent) by Martindale-Hubbell? Are you rated 10.0 (superb) by Avvo? Does your firm have an A+ rating (highest) with the BBB?
- ✓ How much of your practice is devoted to criminal defense?
- ✓ Do you have substantial experience in DUI defense specifically? Because actual results matter, how many DUI cases have you successfully defended?
- ✓ What is it that qualifies you to handle my defense?
- ✓ How good are you at negotiating with the prosecution?
- ✓ Are you a trial lawyer? How many DUI misdemeanor or DUI felony cases have you actually tried? How many of those were jury trials?

- ✓ Do you have substantial experience with DUI sentencing and Arizona's DUI sentencing guidelines?
- ✓ Were you ever a prosecutor? Was that in Arizona or some other jurisdiction? Where in Arizona? How many years were you a prosecutor with the county attorney's office? Did you prosecute DUIs and serious vehicular crimes? What special training did you receive?
- ✓ How familiar are you with this jurisdiction and this courthouse? Do you know the judge assigned to my case? Have you appeared before this judge as defense counsel in another DUI case? Have you appeared before this judge in the past as a prosecutor?
- ✓ Have you ever been sanctioned for an attorney ethics violation?
- ✓ Why are you the most qualified attorney to handle my DUI defense?
- ✓ If I hire your firm, will you handle my DUI defense or will I be turned over to another attorney with the firm?
- ✓ Will you appear beside me in court at all of the criminal proceedings? Will a different attorney with the firm be in court with me? Can I interview that attorney before deciding whether to hire your law firm?

- ✓ How much will the legal representation cost me? How much do you charge if the case does not go to trial?
- ✓ How full is your caseload? Do you have the time available to do a complete job of handling my defense? Should you have a scheduling conflict, will my case remain a priority?
- ✓ How does your firm handle case management? What professional resources, legal support, staff, and technology does the firm have in place? What assurance can you provide that my case will be handled optimally?
- ✓ Will my calls be returned promptly? How long will it take before I get a call back? Who will help me if you're in court or otherwise unavailable?
- ✓ What kind of payment arrangements can I make with you? Do you offer budgeting options? Do you accept credit card payments? What happens to my case if I fall behind on payments?
- ✓ Can you represent me with an appeal if I am convicted of DUI at trial? How much experience do you have with DUI appeals and appellate court procedures?
- ✓ Will I receive copies of all documents in my case?
- ✓ How will the investigation into the facts of my

case be handled and by whom?

- ✓ Have you received specialized legal or investigative training on the issues involved in my case?
- ✓ Is there anything in my case that you don't have experience with?
- ✓ How experienced are you with felony cases for aggravated DUI?
- ✓ Now that I have told you my story, is my case too difficult given your limited experience with felony DUI?

Lastly, ask yourself this very important question: If you hire this attorney, will you have the confidence you need? Both in the representation and in the legal proceedings ahead? If the answer is No, then keep looking.

Find a qualified DUI defense lawyer soon, so mistakes are not made that cannot be remedied. Know what to expect. Prepare. Have a plan.

Selected Arizona Statutes

§ 28-1321. Implied Consent

A. A person who operates a motor vehicle in this state gives consent, subject to § 4-244, paragraph 34 or § 28-1381, 28-1382 or 28-1383, to a test or tests of the person's blood, breath, urine or other bodily substance for the purpose of determining alcohol concentration or drug content if the person is arrested for any offense arising out of acts alleged to have been committed in violation of this chapter or § 4-244, paragraph 34 while the person was driving or in actual physical control of a motor vehicle while under the influence of intoxicating liquor or drugs. The test or tests chosen by the law enforcement agency shall be administered at the direction of a law enforcement officer having reasonable grounds to believe that the person was driving or in actual physical control of a motor vehicle in this state either:

1. While under the influence of intoxicating liquor or drugs.

2. If the person is under 21 years of age, with spirituous liquor in the person's body.

B. After an arrest a violator shall be requested to submit to and successfully complete any test or tests prescribed by subsection A of this section, and if the violator refuses the violator shall be informed that the violator's license or permit to drive will be suspended or denied for 12 months, or for 2 years for a second or subsequent refusal within a period of 84 months, unless the violator expressly agrees to submit to and successfully completes the test or tests. A failure to expressly agree to the test or successfully complete the test is deemed a refusal. The violator shall also be informed that:

1. If the test results show a blood or breath alcohol concentration of 0.08 or more, if the results show a blood or breath alcohol concentration of 0.04 or more and the violator was driving or in actual physical control of a commercial motor vehicle or if the results show there is any drug defined in § 13-3401 or its metabolite in the person's body and the person does not possess a valid prescription for the drug, the violator's license or permit to drive will be suspended or denied for not less than 90 consecutive days.

2. The violator's driving privilege, license, permit, right to apply for a license or permit or nonresident operating privilege may be issued or reinstated following the period of suspension only if the violator completes alcohol or other drug screening.

C. A person who is dead, unconscious or otherwise in a condition rendering the person incapable of refusal is deemed not to have withdrawn the consent provided by subsection A of this section and the test or tests may be administered, subject to § 4-244, paragraph 34 or § 28-1381, 28-1382 or 28-1383.

D. If a person under arrest refuses to submit to the test designated by the law enforcement agency as provided in subsection A of this section:

1. The test shall not be given, except as provided in § 28-1388, subsection E or pursuant to a search warrant.

2. The law enforcement officer directing the administration of the test shall:

(a) File a certified report of the refusal with the department.

(b) On behalf of the department, serve an order of suspension on the person that is effective 15 days after the date the order is served.

(c) Require the immediate surrender of any license or permit to drive that is issued by this state and that is in the possession or control of the person.

(d) If the license or permit is not surrendered, state the reason why it is not surrendered.

(e) If a valid license or permit is surrendered, issue a temporary driving permit that is valid for 15 days.

(f) Forward the certified report of refusal, a copy of the completed notice of suspension, a copy of any completed temporary permit and any driver license or permit taken into possession under this section to the department within 5 days after the issuance of the notice of suspension.

E. The certified report is subject to the penalty for perjury as prescribed by § 28-1561 and shall state all of the following:

1. The officer's reasonable grounds to believe that the arrested person was driving or in actual physical

control of a motor vehicle in this state either:

(a) While under the influence of intoxicating liquor or drugs.

(b) If the person is under 21 years of age, with spirituous liquor in the person's body.

2. The manner in which the person refused to submit to the test or tests.

3. That the person was advised of the consequences of refusal.

F. On receipt of the certified report of refusal and a copy of the order of suspension and on the effective date stated on the order, the department shall enter the order of suspension on its records unless a written or online request for a hearing as provided in this section has been filed by the accused person. If the department receives only the certified report of refusal, the department shall notify the person named in the report in writing sent by mail that:

1. Fifteen days after the date of issuance of the notice the department will suspend the person's license or permit, driving privilege or nonresident driving privilege.

2. The department will provide an opportunity for a hearing if the person requests a hearing in writing or online and the request is received by the department within fifteen days after the notice is sent.

G. The order of suspension issued by a law enforcement officer or the department under this section shall notify the person that:

1. The person may submit a written or online request for a hearing.

2. The request for a hearing must be received by the department within 15 days after the date of the notice or the order of suspension will become final.

3. The affected person's license or permit to drive or right to apply for a license or permit or any nonresident operating privilege will be suspended for 12 months from that date or for 2 years from that date for a second or subsequent refusal within a period of 84 months.

4. The person's driving privilege, license, permit, right to apply for a license or permit or nonresident operating privilege may be issued or reinstated following the period of suspension only if the person completes alcohol or other drug screening.

H. The order for suspension shall:

1. Be accompanied by printed forms that are ready to mail to the department, that may be filled out and signed by the person to indicate the person's desire for a hearing and that advise the person that the person may alternatively submit an online request for a hearing.

2. Advise the person that unless the person has surrendered any driver license or permit issued by this state the person's hearing request will not be accepted, except that the person may certify pursuant to § 28-3170 that the license or permit is lost or destroyed.

I. On the receipt of a request for a hearing, the department shall set the hearing within 60 days. The department may hold the hearing in person, by telephone or by videoconference. If the department holds the hearing in person, the hearing shall be held in the county in which the person named in the report resides unless the law enforcement agency filing the certified report of refusal pursuant to subsection D of this section requests at the time of its filing that the hearing be held in the county where the refusal occurred.

J. A timely request for a hearing stays the suspension until a hearing is held, except that the department shall not return any surrendered license or permit to the person but may issue temporary permits to drive that expire no later than when the department has made its final decision. If the person is a resident without a license or permit or has an expired license or permit, the department may allow the person to apply for a restricted license or permit. If the department determines the person is otherwise entitled to the license or permit, the department shall issue and retain a restricted license or permit subject to this section.

K. Hearings requested under this section shall be conducted in the same manner and under the same conditions as provided in § 28-3306. For the purposes of this section, the scope of the hearing shall include only the issues of whether:

1. A law enforcement officer had reasonable grounds to believe that the person was driving or was in actual physical control of a motor vehicle in this state either:

(a) While under the influence of intoxicating liquor or drugs.

(b) If the person is under 21 years of age, with spirituous liquor in the person's body.

2. The person was placed under arrest.

3. The person refused to submit to the test.

4. The person was informed of the consequences of refusal.

L. If the department determines at the hearing to suspend the affected person's privilege to operate a motor vehicle, the suspension provided in this section is effective 15 days after giving written notice of the suspension, except that the department may issue or extend a temporary license that expires on the effective date of the suspension. If the person is a resident without a license or permit or has an expired license or permit to operate a motor vehicle in this state, the department shall deny to the person the issuance of a license or permit for a period of 12 months after the order of suspension becomes effective or for a period of 2 years after the order of suspension becomes effective for a second or subsequent refusal within a period of 84 months, and may reinstate the person's driving privilege, license, permit, right to apply for a license or permit or nonresident operating privilege following the period of suspension only if the person completes alcohol or other drug screening.

M. If the suspension order is sustained after the hearing, a motion for rehearing is not required. Within 30 days after a suspension order is sustained, the affected person may file a petition in the superior court to review the final order of suspension or denial by the department in the same manner provided in § 28-3317. The court shall hear the review of the final order of suspension or denial on an expedited basis.

N. If the suspension or determination that there should be a denial of issuance is not sustained, the ruling is not admissible in and has no effect on any administrative, civil or criminal court proceeding.

O. If it has been determined under the procedures of this section that a nonresident's privilege to operate a motor vehicle in this state has been suspended, the department shall give information either in writing or by electronic means of the action taken to the motor vehicle administrator of the state of the person's residence and of any state in which the person has a license.

P. After completing not less than 90 consecutive days of the period of suspension required by this section and any alcohol or other drug screening that is ordered by the department pursuant to this chapter, a person whose driving privilege is suspended pursuant to this section may apply to the department for a special ignition interlock restricted driver license pursuant to § 28-1401. Unless the certified ignition interlock period is extended by the department pursuant to § 28-1461, a person who is issued a special ignition interlock restricted driver license as provided in this subsection shall maintain a functioning certified ignition interlock device in compliance with this chapter during the remaining period of the suspension prescribed by this section. This subsection does not apply to a person whose driving privilege is suspended for a second or subsequent refusal within a period of 84 months.

§ 28-1322. Preliminary Breath Tests

A. A law enforcement officer who has reasonable suspicion to believe that a person has committed a violation of § 28-1381 or 28-1382 may request that the person submit to a preliminary breath test or tests before an arrest.

B. In addition to a breath test or tests, the officer may require that the person submit to further testing pursuant to § 28-1321.

C. The director of the department of public safety shall adopt rules prescribing the approval of quantitative preliminary breath testing devices.

§ 28-1381. Driving or Actual Physical Control While Under the Influence

A. It is unlawful for a person to drive or be in actual physical control of a vehicle in this state under any of the following circumstances:

1. While under the influence of intoxicating liquor, any drug, a vapor releasing substance containing a toxic substance or any combination of liquor, drugs or vapor releasing substances if the person is impaired to the slightest degree.

2. If the person has an alcohol concentration of 0.08 or more within 2 hours of driving or being in actual physical control of the vehicle and the alcohol concentration results from alcohol consumed either before or while driving or being in actual physical control of the vehicle.

3. While there is any drug defined in § 13-3401 or its metabolite in the person's body.

4. If the vehicle is a commercial motor vehicle that requires a person to obtain a commercial driver license as defined in § 28-3001 and the person has an alcohol concentration of 0.04 or more.

B. It is not a defense to a charge of a violation of subsection A, paragraph 1 of this section that the person is or has been entitled to use the drug under the laws of this state.

C. A person who is convicted of a violation of this section is guilty of a class 1 misdemeanor.

D. A person using a drug as prescribed by a medical practitioner who is licensed pursuant to title 32 and who is authorized to prescribe the drug is not guilty of violating subsection A, paragraph 3 of this section.

E. In any prosecution for a violation of this section, the state shall allege, for the purpose of classification and sentencing pursuant to this section, all prior convictions of violating this section, § 28-1382 or § 28-1383 occurring within the past 36 months, unless there is an insufficient legal or factual basis to do so.

F. At the arraignment, the court shall inform the

defendant that the defendant may request a trial by jury and that the request, if made, shall be granted.

G. In a trial, action or proceeding for a violation of this section or § 28-1383 other than a trial, action or proceeding involving driving or being in actual physical control of a commercial vehicle, the defendant's alcohol concentration within 2 hours of the time of driving or being in actual physical control as shown by analysis of the defendant's blood, breath or other bodily substance gives rise to the following presumptions:

1. If there was at that time 0.05 or less alcohol concentration in the defendant's blood, breath or other bodily substance, it may be presumed that the defendant was not under the influence of intoxicating liquor.

2. If there was at that time in excess of 0.05 but less than 0.08 alcohol concentration in the defendant's blood, breath or other bodily substance, that fact shall not give rise to a presumption that the defendant was or was not under the influence of intoxicating liquor, but that fact may be considered with other competent evidence in determining the guilt or innocence of the defendant.

3. If there was at that time 0.08 or more alcohol concentration in the defendant's blood, breath or other bodily substance, it may be presumed that the defendant was under the influence of intoxicating liquor.

H. Subsection G of this section does not limit the introduction of any other competent evidence bearing on the question of whether or not the defendant was under the influence of intoxicating liquor.

I. A person who is convicted of a violation of this section:

1. Shall be sentenced to serve not less than 10 consecutive days in jail and is not eligible for probation or suspension of execution of sentence unless the entire sentence is served.

2. Shall pay a fine of not less than 250 dollars.

3. May be ordered by a court to perform community restitution.

4. Shall pay an additional assessment of 500 dollars to be deposited by the state treasurer in the prison construction and operations fund established by § 41-1651. This assessment is not subject to any surcharge. If the conviction occurred in the superior court or a justice court, the court shall transmit the assessed monies to the county treasurer. If the conviction occurred in a municipal court, the court shall transmit the assessed monies to the city treasurer. The city or county treasurer shall transmit the monies received to the state treasurer.

5. Shall pay an additional assessment of 500 dollars to be deposited by the state treasurer in the public safety equipment fund established by § 41-1723. This assessment is not subject to any surcharge. If the conviction occurred in the superior court or a justice court, the court shall transmit the assessed monies to the county treasurer. If the conviction occurred in a municipal court, the court shall transmit the assessed

monies to the city treasurer. The city or county treasurer shall transmit the monies received to the state treasurer.

6. If the violation involved intoxicating liquor, shall be required by the department, on report of the conviction, to equip any motor vehicle the person operates with a certified ignition interlock device pursuant to § 28-3319. In addition, the court may order the person to equip any motor vehicle the person operates with a certified ignition interlock device for more than 12 months beginning on the date of reinstatement of the person's driving privilege following a suspension or revocation or on the date of the department's receipt of the report of conviction, whichever occurs later. The person who operates a motor vehicle with a certified ignition interlock device under this paragraph shall comply with article 5 of this chapter.

J. Notwithstanding subsection I, paragraph 1 of this section, at the time of sentencing the judge may suspend all but one day of the sentence if the person completes a court ordered alcohol or other drug screening, education or treatment program. If the person fails to complete the court ordered alcohol or other drug screening, education or treatment program and has not been placed on probation, the court shall issue an order to show cause to the defendant as to why the remaining jail sentence should not be served.

K. If within a period of 84 months a person is convicted of a second violation of this section or is convicted of a violation of this section and has previously been convicted of a violation of § 28-1382 or 28-1383 or an act in another jurisdiction that if committed in this state would be a violation of this section or § 28-1382 or 28-1383, the person:

1. Shall be sentenced to serve not less than 90 days in jail, 30 days of which shall be served consecutively, and is not eligible for probation or suspension of execution of sentence unless the entire sentence has been served.

2. Shall pay a fine of not less than 500 dollars.

3. Shall be ordered by a court to perform at least 30 hours of community restitution.

4. Shall have the person's driving privilege revoked for one year. The court shall report the conviction to the department. On receipt of the report, the department shall revoke the person's driving privilege and, if the violation involved intoxicating liquor, shall require the person to equip any motor vehicle the person operates with a certified ignition interlock device pursuant to § 28-3319. In addition, the court may order the person to equip any motor vehicle the person operates with a certified ignition interlock device for more than 12 months beginning on the date of reinstatement of the person's driving privilege following a suspension or revocation or on the date of the department's receipt of the report of conviction, whichever occurs later. The person who operates a motor vehicle with a certified ignition interlock device under this paragraph shall comply

with article 5 of this chapter.

5. Shall pay an additional assessment of 1,250 dollars to be deposited by the state treasurer in the prison construction and operations fund established by § 41-1651. This assessment is not subject to any surcharge. If the conviction occurred in the superior court or a justice court, the court shall transmit the assessed monies to the county treasurer. If the conviction occurred in a municipal court, the court shall transmit the assessed monies to the city treasurer. The city or county treasurer shall transmit the monies received to the state treasurer.

6. Shall pay an additional assessment of 1,250 dollars to be deposited by the state treasurer in the public safety equipment fund established by § 41-1723. This assessment is not subject to any surcharge. If the conviction occurred in the superior court or a justice court, the court shall transmit the assessed monies to the county treasurer. If the conviction occurred in a municipal court, the court shall transmit the assessed monies to the city treasurer. The city or county treasurer shall transmit the monies received to the state treasurer.

L. Notwithstanding subsection K, paragraph 1 of this section, at the time of sentencing, the judge may suspend all but 30 days of the sentence if the person completes a court ordered alcohol or other drug screening, education or treatment program. If the person fails to complete the court ordered alcohol or other drug screening, education or treatment program and has not been placed on probation, the court shall issue an order to show cause as to why the remaining jail sentence should not be served.

M. In applying the 84 month provision of subsection K of this section, the dates of the commission of the offense shall be the determining factor, irrespective of the sequence in which the offenses were committed.

N. A second violation for which a conviction occurs as provided in this section shall not include a conviction for an offense arising out of the same series of acts.

O. After completing 45 days of the revocation period prescribed by subsection K of this section, a person whose driving privilege is revoked for a violation of this section and who is sentenced pursuant to subsection K of this section is eligible for a special ignition interlock restricted driver license pursuant to § 28-1401.

P. The court may order a person who is convicted of a violation of this section that does not involve intoxicating liquor to equip any motor vehicle the person operates with a certified ignition interlock device pursuant to § 28-3319. On report of the conviction and certified ignition interlock device requirement, the department shall require the person to equip any motor vehicle the person operates with a certified ignition interlock device pursuant to § 28-3319. In addition, the court may order the person to equip any motor vehicle the person operates with a certified ignition interlock device for more than 12 months beginning on the date of reinstatement of the person's driving privilege following a suspension or revocation or on the date of the department's receipt of the report of conviction, whichever occurs later.

The person who operates a motor vehicle with a certified ignition interlock device under this subsection shall comply with article 5 of this chapter.

§ 28-1382. Driving or Actual Physical Control While Under the Extreme Influence of Intoxicating Liquor

A. It is unlawful for a person to drive or be in actual physical control of a vehicle in this state if the person has an alcohol concentration as follows within 2 hours of driving or being in actual physical control of the vehicle and the alcohol concentration results from alcohol consumed either before or while driving or being in actual physical control of the vehicle:

1. 0.15 or more but less than 0.20.

2. 0.20 or more.

B. A person who is convicted of a violation of this section is guilty of driving or being in actual physical control of a vehicle while under the extreme influence of intoxicating liquor.

C. At the arraignment, the court shall inform the defendant that the defendant may request a trial by jury and that the request, if made, shall be granted.

D. A person who is convicted of a violation of this section:

1. Shall be sentenced to serve not less than 30 consecutive days in jail and is not eligible for probation or suspension of execution of sentence unless the entire sentence is served if the person is convicted of a

violation of subsection A, paragraph 1 of this section. A person who is convicted of a violation of subsection A, paragraph 2 of this section shall be sentenced to serve not less than 45 consecutive days in jail and is not eligible for probation or suspension of execution of sentence unless the entire sentence is served.

2. Shall pay a fine of not less than 250 dollars, except that a person who is convicted of a violation of subsection A, paragraph 2 of this section shall pay a fine of not less than 500 dollars.

The fine prescribed in this paragraph and any assessments, restitution and incarceration costs shall be paid before the assessment prescribed in paragraph 3 of this subsection.

3. Shall pay an additional assessment of 250 dollars. If the conviction occurred in the superior court or a justice court, the court shall transmit the monies received pursuant to this paragraph to the county treasurer. If the conviction occurred in a municipal court, the court shall transmit the monies received pursuant to this paragraph to the city treasurer. The city or county treasurer shall transmit the monies received to the state treasurer. The state treasurer shall deposit the monies received in the driving under the influence abatement fund established by § 28-1304.

4. May be ordered by a court to perform community restitution.

5. Shall be required by the department, on receipt of the report of conviction, to equip any motor vehicle the person operates with a certified ignition interlock

device pursuant to § 28-3319. In addition, the court may order the person to equip any motor vehicle the person operates with a certified ignition interlock device for more than 12 months beginning on the date of reinstatement of the person's driving privilege following a suspension or revocation or on the date of the department's receipt of the report of conviction, whichever occurs later. The person who operates a motor vehicle with a certified ignition interlock device under this paragraph shall comply with article 5 of this chapter.

6. Shall pay an additional assessment of 1,000 dollars to be deposited by the state treasurer in the prison construction and operations fund established by § 41-1651. This assessment is not subject to any surcharge. If the conviction occurred in the superior court or a justice court, the court shall transmit the assessed monies to the county treasurer. If the conviction occurred in a municipal court, the court shall transmit the assessed monies to the city treasurer. The city or county treasurer shall transmit the monies received to the state treasurer.

7. Shall pay an additional assessment of 1,000 dollars to be deposited by the state treasurer in the public safety equipment fund established by § 41-1723. This assessment is not subject to any surcharge. If the conviction occurred in the superior court or a justice court, the court shall transmit the assessed monies to the county treasurer. If the conviction occurred in a municipal court, the court shall transmit the assessed

monies to the city treasurer. The city or county treasurer shall transmit the monies received to the state treasurer.

E. If within a period of 84 months a person is convicted of a second violation of this section or is convicted of a violation of this section and has previously been convicted of a violation of § 28-1381 or 28-1383 or an act in another jurisdiction that if committed in this state would be a violation of this section or § 28-1381 or 28-1383, the person:

1. Shall be sentenced to serve not less than 120 days in jail, 60 days of which shall be served consecutively, and is not eligible for probation or suspension of execution of sentence unless the entire sentence has been served if the person is convicted of a violation of subsection A, paragraph 1 of this section. A person who is convicted of a violation of subsection A, paragraph 2 of this section shall be sentenced to serve not less than 180 days in jail, 90 of which shall be served consecutively, and is not eligible for probation or suspension of execution of sentence unless the entire sentence has been served.

2. Shall pay a fine of not less than 500 dollars, except that a person who is convicted of a violation of subsection A, paragraph 2 of this section shall pay a fine of not less than 1,000 dollars. The fine prescribed in this paragraph and any assessments, restitution and incarceration costs shall be paid before the assessment prescribed in paragraph 3 of this subsection.

3. Shall pay an additional assessment of 250 dollars. If the conviction occurred in the superior court or a justice court, the court shall transmit the monies received pursuant to this paragraph to the county treasurer. If the conviction occurred in a municipal court, the court shall transmit the monies received pursuant to this paragraph to the city treasurer. The city or county treasurer shall transmit the monies received to the state treasurer. The state treasurer shall deposit the monies received in the driving under the influence abatement fund established by § 28-1304.

4. Shall be ordered by a court to perform at least 30 hours of community restitution.

5. Shall have the person's driving privilege revoked for at least one year. The court shall report the conviction to the department. On receipt of the report, the department shall revoke the person's driving privilege and shall require the person to equip any motor vehicle the person operates with a certified ignition interlock device pursuant to § 28-3319. In addition, the court may order the person to equip any motor vehicle the person operates with a certified ignition interlock device for more than 12 months beginning on the date of reinstatement of the person's driving privilege following a suspension or revocation or on the date of the department's receipt of the report of conviction, whichever is later. The person who operates a motor vehicle with a certified ignition interlock device under this paragraph shall comply with article 5 of this chapter.

6. Shall pay an additional assessment of 1,250 dollars to be deposited by the state treasurer in the prison construction and operations fund established by § 41-1651. This assessment is not subject to any surcharge. If the conviction occurred in the superior court or a justice court, the court shall transmit the assessed monies to the county treasurer. If the conviction occurred in a municipal court, the court shall transmit the assessed monies to the city treasurer. The city or county treasurer shall transmit the monies received to the state treasurer.

7. Shall pay an additional assessment of 1,250 dollars to be deposited by the state treasurer in the public safety equipment fund established by § 41-1723. This assessment is not subject to any surcharge. If the conviction occurred in the superior court or a justice court, the court shall transmit the assessed monies to the county treasurer. If the conviction occurred in a municipal court, the court shall transmit the assessed monies to the city treasurer. The city or county treasurer shall transmit the monies received to the state treasurer.

F. In applying the 84 month provision of subsection E of this section, the dates of the commission of the offense shall be the determining factor, irrespective of the sequence in which the offenses were committed.

G. A second violation for which a conviction occurs as provided in this section shall not include a conviction for an offense arising out of the same series of acts.

H. After completing 45 days of the revocation period

prescribed by subsection E of this section, a person whose driving privilege is revoked for a violation of this section and who is sentenced pursuant to subsection E of this section is eligible for a special ignition interlock restricted driver license pursuant to § 28-1401.

I. Notwithstanding subsection D, paragraph 1 of this section, at the time of sentencing if the person is convicted of a violation of subsection A, paragraph 1 of this section, the judge may suspend all but 9 days of the sentence if the person equips any motor vehicle the person operates with a certified ignition interlock device for a period of 12 months. If the person is convicted of a violation of subsection A, paragraph 2 of this section, the judge may suspend all but 14 days of the sentence if the person equips any motor vehicle the person operates with a certified ignition interlock device for a period of 12 months. If the person fails to comply with article 5 of this chapter and has not been placed on probation, the court shall issue an order to show cause as to why the remaining jail sentence should not be served.

J. A person who is convicted of a violation of this section is guilty of a class 1 misdemeanor.

§ 28-1383. Aggravated Driving

A. A person is guilty of aggravated driving or actual physical control while under the influence of intoxicating liquor or drugs if the person does any of the following:

1. Commits a violation of § 28-1381, § 28-1382 or this section while the person's driver license or privilege

to drive is suspended, canceled, revoked or refused or while a restriction is placed on the person's driver license or privilege to drive as a result of violating § 28-1381 or 28-1382 or under § 28-1385.

2. Within a period of 84 months commits a third or subsequent violation of § 28-1381, § 28-1382 or this section or is convicted of a violation of § 28-1381, § 28-1382 or this section and has previously been convicted of any combination of convictions of § 28-1381, § 28-1382 or this section or acts in another jurisdiction that if committed in this state would be a violation of § 28-1381, § 28-1382 or this section.

3. While a person under 15 years of age is in the vehicle, commits a violation of either:

(a) § 28-1381.

(b) § 28-1382.

4. While the person is ordered by the court or required pursuant to § 28-3319 by the department to equip any motor vehicle the person operates with a certified ignition interlock device, commits a violation of § 28-1381, § 28-1382 or this section.

B. The dates of the commission of the offenses are the determining factor in applying the 84 month provision provided in subsection A, paragraph 2 of this section regardless of the sequence in which the offenses were committed. For the purposes of this section, a third or subsequent violation for which a conviction occurs does not include a conviction for an offense arising out of the same series of acts. The time that a probationer is found to be on absconder status or the time that a person is incarcerated in any state, federal, county or city jail or correctional facility is excluded when determining the 84 month period provided in subsection A, paragraph 2 and subsection E of this section.

C. The notice to a person of the suspension, cancellation, revocation or refusal of a driver license or privilege to drive is effective as provided in § 28-3318 or pursuant to the laws of the state issuing the license.

D. A person is not eligible for probation, pardon, commutation or suspension of sentence or release on any other basis until the person has served not less than 4 months in prison if the person is convicted under either of the following:

1. Subsection A, paragraph 1 of this section.

2. Subsection A, paragraph 2 of this section and within an 84 month period has been convicted of two prior violations of § 28-1381, § 28-1382 or this section, or any combination of those sections, or acts in another jurisdiction that if committed in this state would be a violation of § 28-1381, § 28-1382 or this section.

E. A person who is convicted under subsection A, paragraph 2 of this section and who within an 84 month period has been convicted of three or more prior violations of § 28-1381, § 28-1382 or this section, or any combination of those sections, or acts in another jurisdiction that if committed in this state would be a violation of § 28-1381, § 28-1382 or this section is not eligible for probation, pardon, commutation or suspension of sentence or release on any other basis until the person has served not less than 8 months in prison.

F. A person who is convicted under subsection A, paragraph 3, subdivision (a) of this section shall serve at least the minimum term of incarceration required pursuant to § 28-1381.

G. A person who is convicted under subsection A, paragraph 3, subdivision (b) of this section shall serve at least the minimum term of incarceration required pursuant to § 28-1382.

H. A person who is convicted of a violation of this section shall attend and complete alcohol or other drug screening, education or treatment from an approved facility. If the person fails to comply with this subsection and is placed on probation, in addition to the provisions of § 13-901 the court may order that the person be incarcerated as a term of probation as follows:

1. For a person sentenced pursuant to subsection D of this section, for an individual period of not more than 4 months and a total period of not more than one year.

2. For a person sentenced pursuant to subsection E of this section, for an individual period of not more than 8 months and a total period of not more than 2 years.

I. The time that a person spends in custody pursuant to subsection H of this section shall not be counted towards the sentence imposed if the person's probation is revoked and the person is sentenced to prison after revocation of probation.

J. On a conviction for a violation of this section, the court:

1. Shall report the conviction to the department. On receipt of the report, the department shall revoke the driving privilege of the person. The department shall not issue the person a new driver license within one year of the date of the conviction and, if the violation involved intoxicating liquor, shall require the person to equip any motor vehicle the person operates with a certified ignition interlock device pursuant to § 28-3319. In addition, the court may order the person to equip any motor vehicle the person operates with a certified ignition interlock device for more than 24 months beginning on the date of reinstatement of the person's driving privilege following a suspension or revocation or on the date of the department's receipt of the report of conviction, whichever occurs later. The person who operates a motor vehicle with a certified ignition interlock device under this paragraph shall comply with article 5 of this chapter.

2. In addition to any other penalty prescribed by law, shall order the person to pay an additional assessment of 250 dollars. If the conviction occurred in the superior court or a justice court, the court shall transmit the monies received pursuant to this paragraph to the county treasurer. If the conviction occurred in a municipal court, the court shall transmit the monies received pursuant to this paragraph to the city treasurer. The city or county treasurer shall transmit the monies received to the state treasurer.

The state treasurer shall deposit the monies received in the driving under the influence abatement fund established by § 28-1304. Any fine imposed for a violation of this section and any assessments, restitution and incarceration costs shall be paid before the assessment prescribed in this paragraph.

3. Shall order the person to pay a fine of not less than 750 dollars.

4. In addition to any other penalty prescribed by law, shall order the person to pay an additional assessment of 1,500 dollars to be deposited by the state treasurer in the prison construction and operations fund established by § 41-1651. This assessment is not subject to any surcharge. If the conviction occurred in the superior court or a justice court, the court shall transmit the assessed monies to the county treasurer. If the conviction occurred in a municipal court, the court shall transmit the assessed monies to the city treasurer. The city or county treasurer shall transmit the monies received to the state treasurer.

5. In addition to any other penalty prescribed by law, shall order the person to pay an additional assessment of 1,500 dollars to be deposited by the state treasurer in the public safety equipment fund established by § 41-1723. This assessment is not subject to any surcharge. If the conviction occurred in the superior court or a justice court, the court shall transmit the assessed monies to the county treasurer. If the conviction occurred in a municipal court, the court shall transmit the assessed monies to the city

treasurer. The city or county treasurer shall transmit the monies received to the state treasurer.

K. After completing the period of suspension required by § 28-1385, a person whose driving privilege is revoked for a violation of subsection A, paragraph 3 of this section may apply to the department for a special ignition interlock restricted driver license pursuant to § 28-1401.

L. The court may order a person who is convicted of a violation of this section that does not involve intoxicating liquor to equip any motor vehicle the person operates with a certified ignition interlock device pursuant to § 28-3319. On report of the conviction and certified ignition interlock device requirement, the department shall require the person to equip any motor vehicle the person operates with a certified ignition interlock device pursuant to § 28-3319. In addition, the court may order the person to equip any motor vehicle the person operates with a certified ignition interlock device for more than 12 months beginning on the date of reinstatement of the person's driving privilege following a suspension or revocation or on the date of the department's receipt of the report of conviction, whichever occurs later. The person who operates a motor vehicle with a certified ignition interlock device under this subsection shall comply with article 5 of this chapter.

M. Aggravated driving or actual physical control while under the influence of intoxicating liquor or drugs committed under:

1. Subsection A, paragraph 1, 2 or 4 of this section is a class 4 felony.

2. Subsection A, paragraph 3 of this section is a class 6 felony.

N. For the purposes of this section, "suspension, cancellation, revocation or refusal" means any suspension, cancellation, revocation or refusal.

§ 28-1384. Aggravated driving or actual physical control while under the influence; forfeiture of vehicle

A. If a person is convicted of violating § 28-1383, the court, in addition to any other penalty imposed by law, shall order the motor vehicle owned and operated by the person at the time of the offense forfeited in the same manner as provided in title 13, chapter 39.

B. A vehicle used by a person as a common carrier in the transaction of business as a common carrier is not subject to forfeiture unless it appears that the owner or other person in charge of the vehicle consented to or was privy to a violation described in subsection A of this section.

C. Property that is subject to forfeiture and all interests in property that are forfeited under this section shall be disposed of and allocated in the same manner as provided in title 13, chapter 39, except that all monies that are obtained as a result of forfeiture under this section shall be deposited in the state general fund.

Scott David Stewart, Esq.

Stewart Law Group opened its doors over a decade ago with a singular focus on the client and that individual's experience dealing with very difficult emotional legal pressures. Since its beginning, this firm has garnered the trust and respect of clients as a distinguished criminal defense firm.

Prior to forming Stewart Law Group, Mr. Stewart worked as a Deputy County Attorney for the Maricopa County Attorney's Office where he served as a Felony Prosecutor and a Vehicular Crimes Prosecutor in the Major Felony Crimes Division. The Vehicular Crimes Bureau prosecutes vehicular homicide, aggravated assault, DUI and aggravated DUI cases. While working as a felony prosecutor, he successfully prosecuted thousands of serious felony crimes, including armed robbery, aggravated assault, dangerous crimes, stabbing, drug sale and possession, auto-theft, burglary, forgery, fraud, and domestic violence.

The Maricopa County Attorney's Office is where Mr. Stewart honed his trial skills and developed strategies for success that he continues to use and implement in his criminal defense practice. His experience as a felony prosecutor opened his eyes to the need for zealous legal representation in defense of those lacking a strong voice against the criminal justice system.

Mr. Stewart is a member in good standing of the State Bar of Arizona, Maricopa County Bar Association, and American Bar Association. He has an AV Preeminent® attorney-rating from Martindale-Hubbell®. His memberships include the National College for DUI Defense, Arizona Attorneys for Criminal Justice, National Association of Criminal Defense Lawyers, and Association of Trial Lawyers of America — Criminal Law Section.

After graduating from Northern Arizona University with a Bachelor's Degree in Speech Communication, Mr. Stewart chose to attend the Illinois Institute of Technology, Chicago-Kent College of Law. Chicago-Kent was his law school of choice because of their renowned reputation for producing trial attorneys, as well as their signature certificate program in Litigation and Alternative Dispute Resolution.

While in law school, Mr. Stewart became a certified mediator with the Center for Conflict Resolution and successfully mediated high conflict landlord tenant disputes for Cook County Circuit Court. He participated in the law school's criminal defense clinic where he, along with several law students and their clinical professor, researched, investigated and uncovered evidence proving a death row inmate's innocence. The law school, the students, and their professor were profiled on the nationally syndicated television show Extra® and numerous other local media news stations. The amazing experience gained while in law school taught Mr. Stewart essential negotiation, litigation, and investigation skills. Skills he utilizes daily in defending clients charged with crimes.

Born and raised in Phoenix, Arizona, Mr. Stewart is a first generation Phoenician with strong ties to the community. The son of a small business owner, he credits his parents for his entrepreneurial spirit and strong emphasis on core values of integrity, respect, responsibility, leadership, work ethic, and family. These are the values that guide him daily in his work representing clients who face difficulties and hardship in the criminal justice system.

Stewart Law Group

777 E Thomas Rd Ste 210, Phoenix AZ 85014
Phone: 602.548.4600

1490 S Price Rd Ste 212, Chandler AZ 85286
14050 N 83rd Ave Ste 290, Peoria AZ 85381
17470 N Pacesetter Way, Scottsdale AZ 85255
2929 N Power Ste 101, Mesa AZ 85215
20325 N 51st Ave Ste 134, Glendale AZ 85308
1166 E Warner Rd Ste 101U, Gilbert AZ 85296

www.ArizonaLawGroup.com

96282836R00083

Made in the USA
Columbia, SC
27 May 2018